AF327284

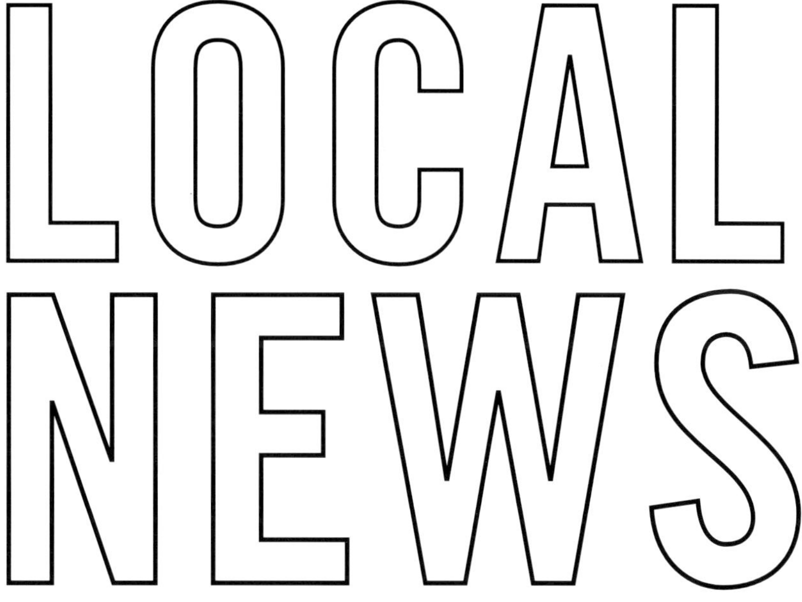

LOCAL NEWS

TABLOID PICTURES FROM THE
LOS ANGELES HERALD EXPRESS 1936–1961

LOCAL

TABLOID PICTURES FROM THE LOS

EDITED BY

A LOOKOUT BOOK

NEWS

ANGELES HERALD EXPRESS 1936–1961

DIANE KEATON

D.A.P./DISTRIBUTED ART PUBLISHERS, INC.

EDITED BY **DIANE**

After the husband she later claimed died deserted her, my Grandmother Hall migrated from Nebraska to California. With her infant son (my father, Jack) and her sister Sadie beside her, they drove to the Promised Land. It was the 20s. No matter what misfortune had befallen them, they were heartlanders with high hopes. L.A. was the place for them.

My father, Jack, would tell me stories about his mother sneaking him into the gambling ships docked off Catalina Island when he was a little boy. They lived in a duplex in Highland Park. Dad played clarinet for Colonel Parker's Marching Band, and Grammy gambled on the weekends.

My mother, Dorothy Keaton, was born in Kansas. Her parents, Beulah and Roy, drifted into L.A. before she was three. They too were heartlanders holding out for the big dream, which dumped them into a little California bungalow in the hills of Harmon Way, right off Monterey Road. My mother played the piano and sang in a trio called Two Dots and a Dash at her high school. She was sixteen when Roy drove off, leaving Beulah and his three daughters to fend for themselves.

KEATON

Dorothy met Jack on a basketball court when she was nineteen and he was twenty. They fell in love and eloped in Las Vegas at the Stardust Hotel. Five years after I was born my father would drive me, every Saturday, to the Department of Water and Power in downtown L.A., where he worked as a civil engineer. From his office I could see Union Station and the trolleys that went up Bunker Hill. Later, we would drive through the Second Street Tunnel to Clifton's Cafeteria, where Dad and I walked through a fake jungle and picked up lime-green jello squares in pretty dishes and put them on our trays.

That's when I realized LOS ANGELES was my town. I belong here. I've always belonged here. My parents belonged here. My grandparents belonged here. Just like the people in this book.

We never got the HERALD EXPRESS. Mom and Dad liked the HIGHLAND PARK NEWS HERALD because it was free. The L. A. TIMES was too expensive and the Herald Express was a Hearst Paper, whatever that meant. The only time I remember seeing the Herald was on Grammy Hall's coffee table in her little Spanish duplex. She loved it. She even had it delivered. She lived to rehash the Herald's coverage of local horror stories. No member of our family will ever forget how Spade Cooley beat his wife to death one April while hopped up on amphetamines.

The Herald Express was read by people who didn't have time to read. Following in the footsteps of William Randolph Hearst's other newspapers, the Herald predictably upheld his formula of short copy, lurid headlines, information as entertainment, and lots of law-and-order messages in the form of moral tales. As Robert Johnson, a Hearst assistant city editor, once remarked, "The paper was aimed at the underside of the community, the barely literate, the bored, the poor, the people who want to know about murders and UFO's and sports results, and damn little else. It was just sloppy. No metro in America had more typos. We were embarrassed to tell people we worked there. It always crawled all over any disaster because they were easy to cover." Aside from the local crime news or trials, most stories in the newspaper were picked up from the wires.

This meant that the Herald had all the more space for—pictures. And it took full advantage of this by jamming its pages with plenty of them. As Hearst himself said, "Illustrations embellish a page, illustrations attract the eye and stimulate the imagination of the lower classes and materially aid the comprehension of an unaccustomed reader."

In a further effort to stimulate the imagination of the paper's readership, Aggie Underwood, the first female city editor of a major metropolitan paper, prided herself on christening murder cases with catchy names. In a moment of inspiration and calculation, she dropped a white carnation (flash) on the body of a waitress who had been stabbed to death, just to be able to name the story "THE WHITE CARNATION MURDER."

It was a strange, serendipitous coincidence that fifteen years after Grammy Hall's death, I found myself in the basement of the L.A. PUBLIC LIBRARY rummaging through the Herald Express photos in the Herald Examiner photographic archive. Out of the 2.2 million forgotten photographs collecting dust, the most compelling were best summed up in two words: LOCAL NEWS, i.e., Murdered Women, Rapists, Suicides, Hold-Up Suspects, Found Dogs, Missing Children, Cross-Dressers, etc.

The Herald offered these accident victims, divorcees, wife beaters, murderers, and others a sort of redemption through a pathetically short-lived fame. It continued to feed its audience (my grandmother) the unfillable black hole of somebody else's misfortune. Certain stories were chronicled in great visual detail. Mother Brink, pregnant with her seventeenth child, was caught passing bad checks. Father Brink, accused by one of his daughters of kidnapping another daughter, was in jail awaiting trial. Their saga was covered for weeks, featuring portraits of the father, portraits of the mother, intimate shots of the family eating in their hovel home or stuffed inside their rickety Model T. Finally the Brinks could be milked no more. The series ended with a well-posed, heartbreaking portrait of the children standing on the Brinks' broken-down porch, with the caption underneath reading, "BRINK CHILDREN WATCH MOMMY GO TO JAIL."

People like "BLIND EX-G.I. EDWARD M. GOODMAN REUNITED WITH HIS SEEING-EYE DOG TRUMP AFTER BEING SEPARATED FOR 2 MONTHS" got his picture in the paper. Gladys Grady got her picture in the paper after she was freed from jail for having worn Marine uniform trousers to a drinking party. My mother's picture was in the paper when she won the Mrs. Los Angeles contest forty years ago.

But Grammy Keaton's picture was never taken, even though she was a hard-luck story who had to hit the streets looking for a job, for the first time, at the age of forty-two. My father's story of being an abandoned kid without a Dad should have been part of the LOCAL NEWS, but no one ever took a picture of little Jack Hall searching for his Daddy. But it belongs in the LOCAL NEWS as surely as the almost forgotten people pictured here do. Who of us hasn't disappeared into the thin air of a lousy marriage, a failed bank account, a petty crime, or drifted into exactly what we never imagined we would become, i.e., preoccupied narcissists, personal injury lawyers, right-wing bigots, common thieves, divorced single women raising children alone, abandoned lovers? Who hasn't found themselves in the seemingly unimaginable position of becoming just one of the millions of ordinary, sad stories that make up life?

Here in L.A., where the impossible is possible, most of us fall in the line of fire, still holding onto our dreams. You may ask yourself, where is the dream in these photographs? To me, it lies in the shiny satin fabric of Beverly Bennett's dress as she tells the police she shot her

husband because he refused to give her money. It lies in the little photograph of Marilyn Monroe resting on the shelf of Frank Rutherford's bookie shop on South Western Avenue. These details are the remnants of the dreams people came to town with. That's what their faces say to me. They say, we're holding on, and yes, it may be a small-minded, idiot's folly that could only come out of L.A. with its lame-o promise of eternal youth, but it's ours.

As the forgotten faces of the LOCAL NEWS, faces that almost never existed, like my father's and his mother's before him, these portraits are a stockpile of neglected treasures. This book honors them; it honors the pretty, the hopeful, the ordinary, the murdered, the ugly, the tortured, the smug, the guilty, the lost and found. Their beauty lies in a transcendent beauty we all share: our common fate. Each human face is a compelling mystery that looks back at us like a mirror reflecting the absolute fact that we live, we die, and we are forgotten. This book is for all of us, your family and mine. This book is for those who slip away unnoticed.

LOST

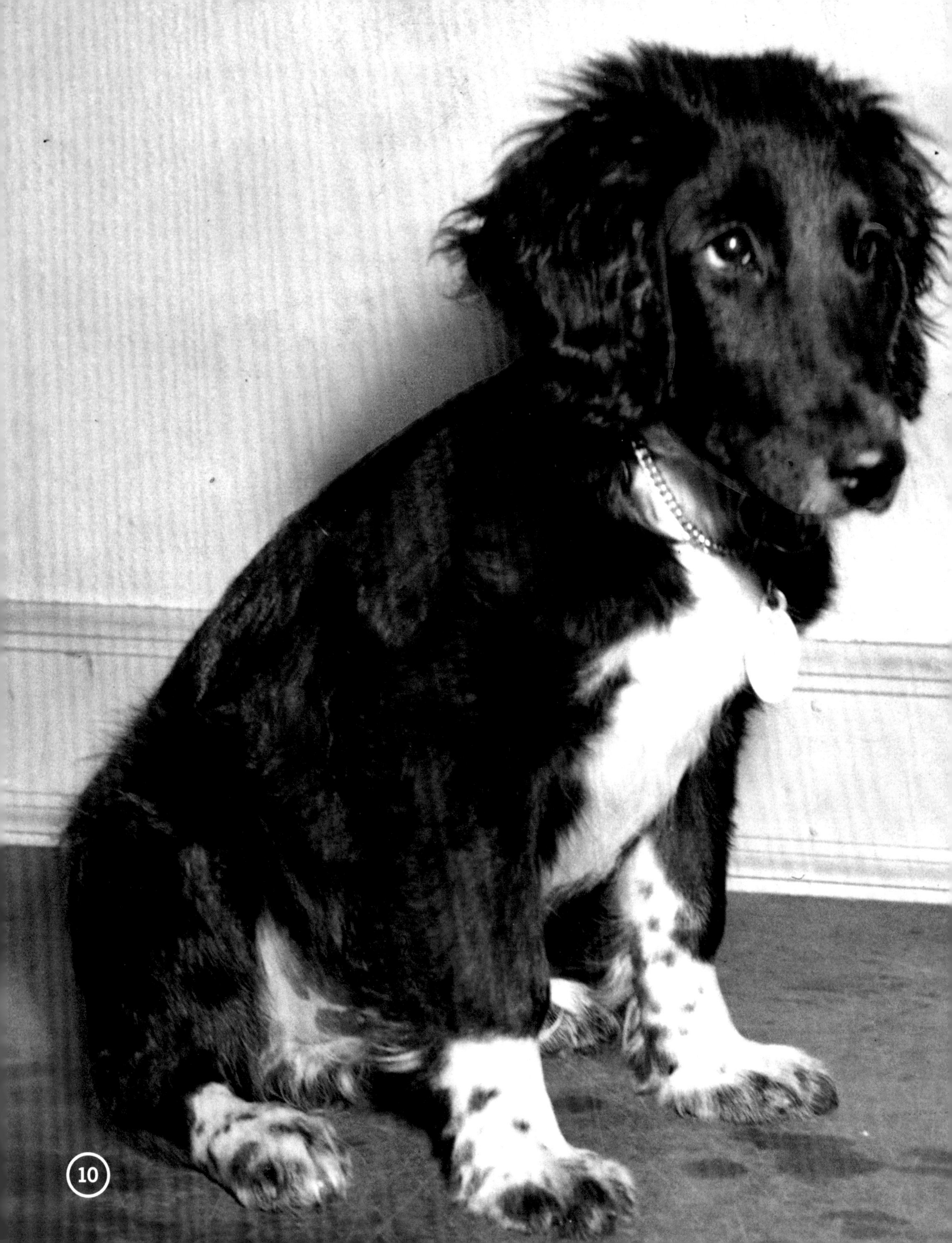

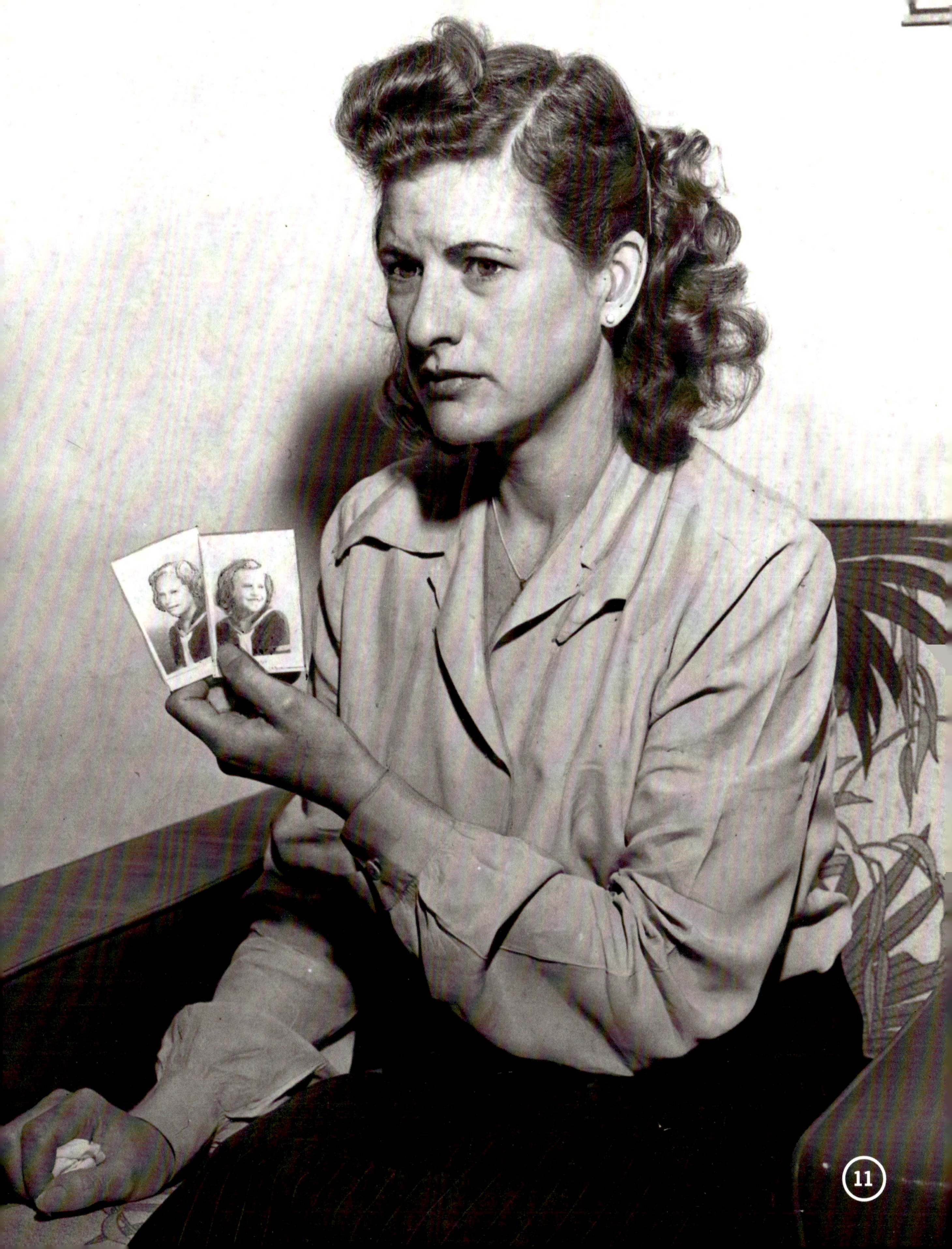

11

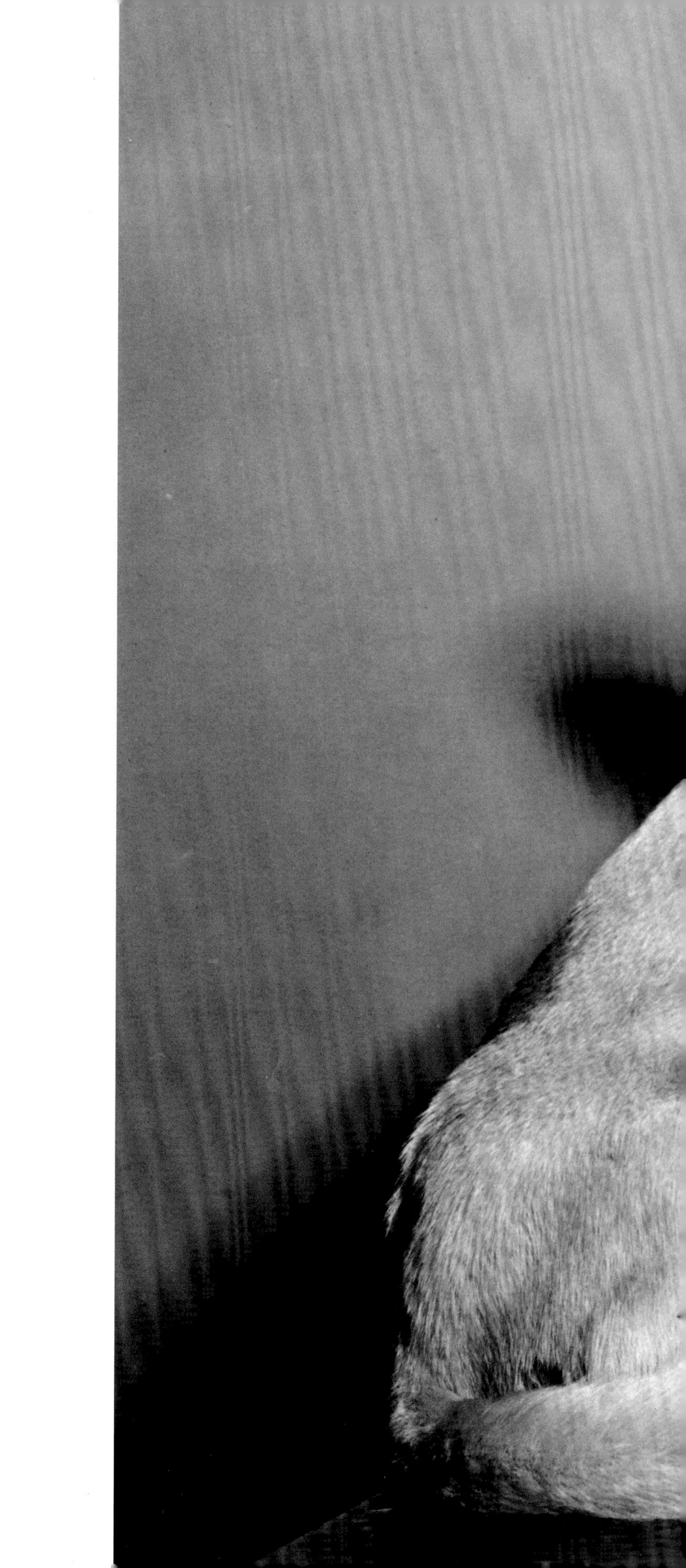

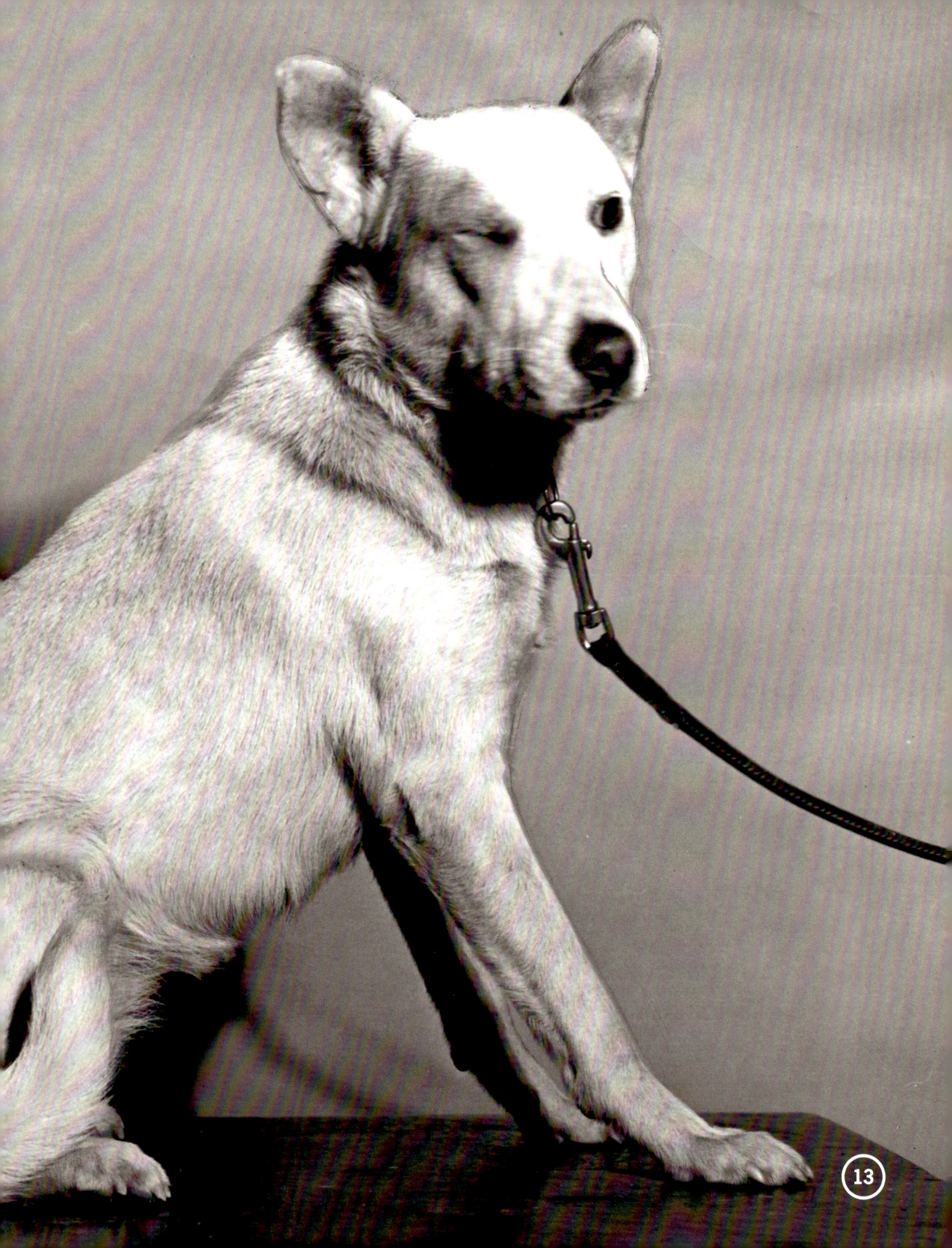

13

SCENE OF

THE CRIME

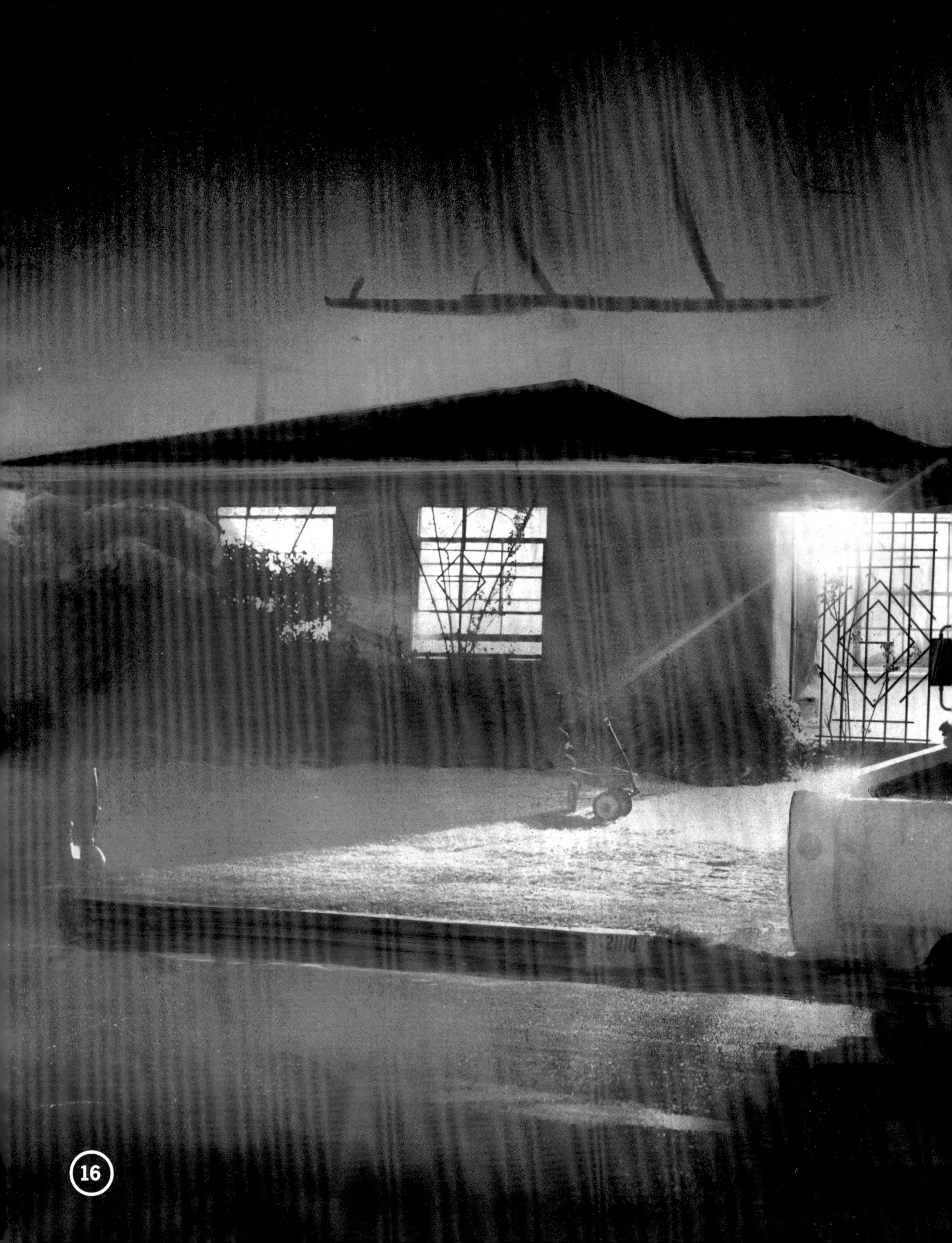

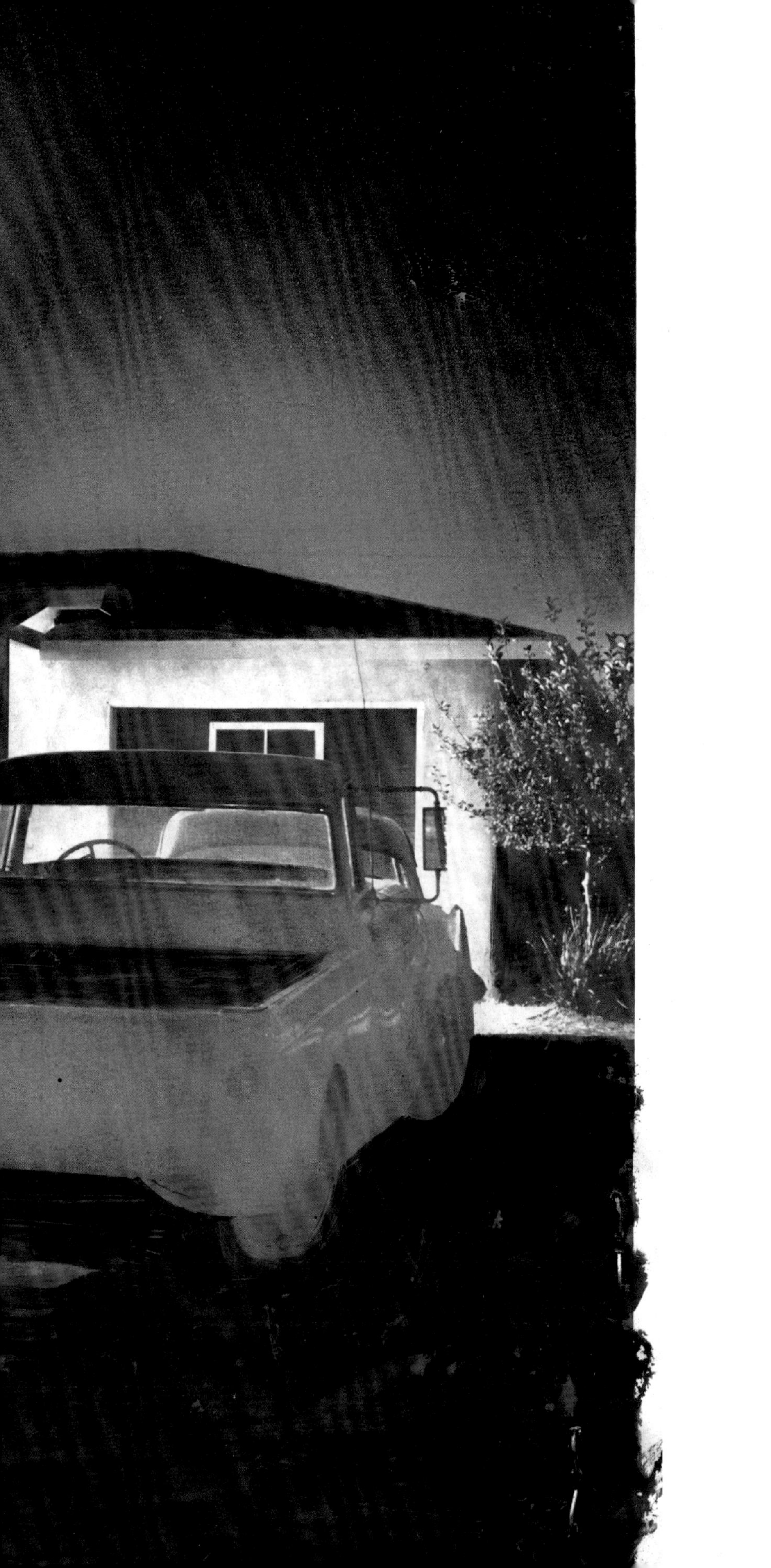

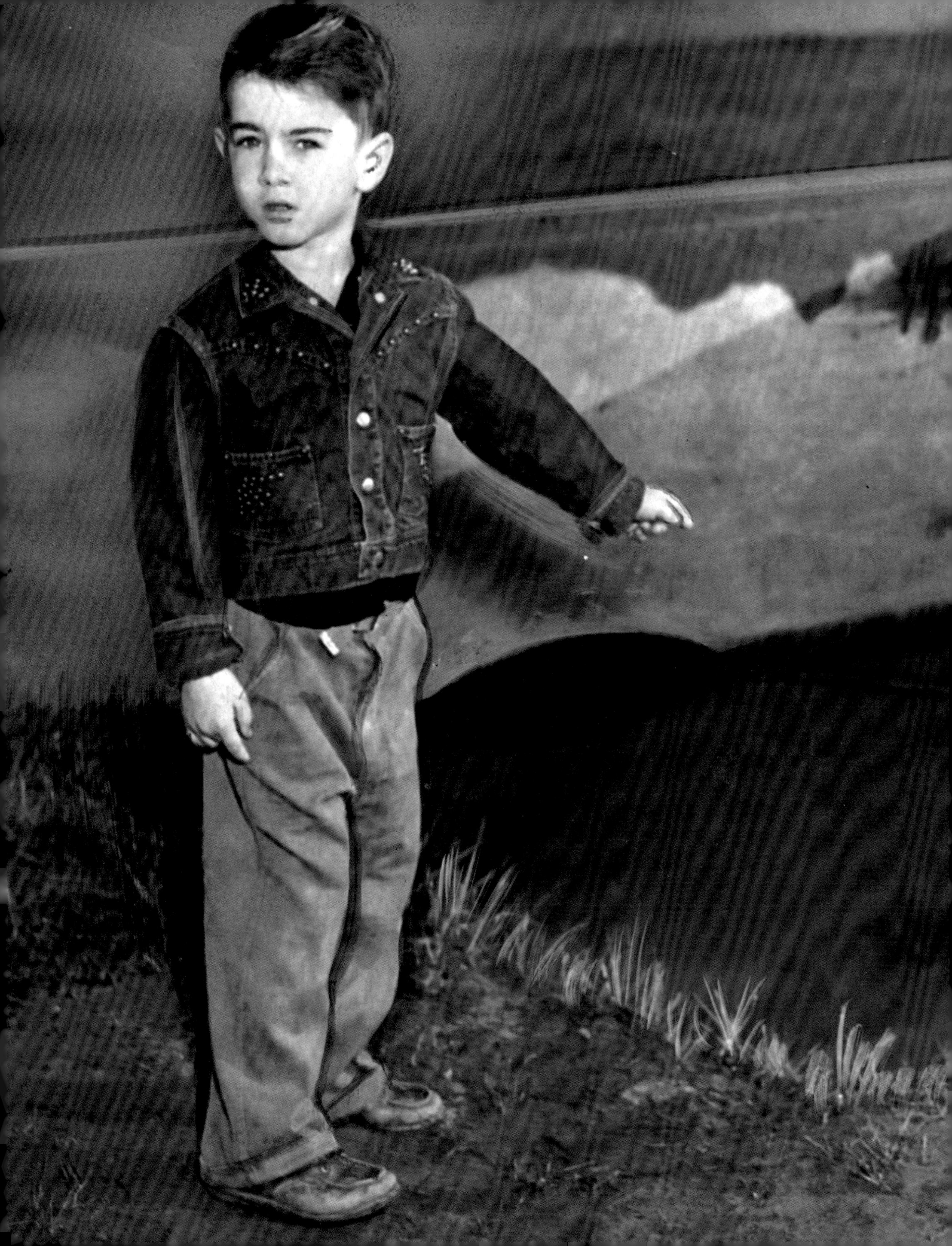

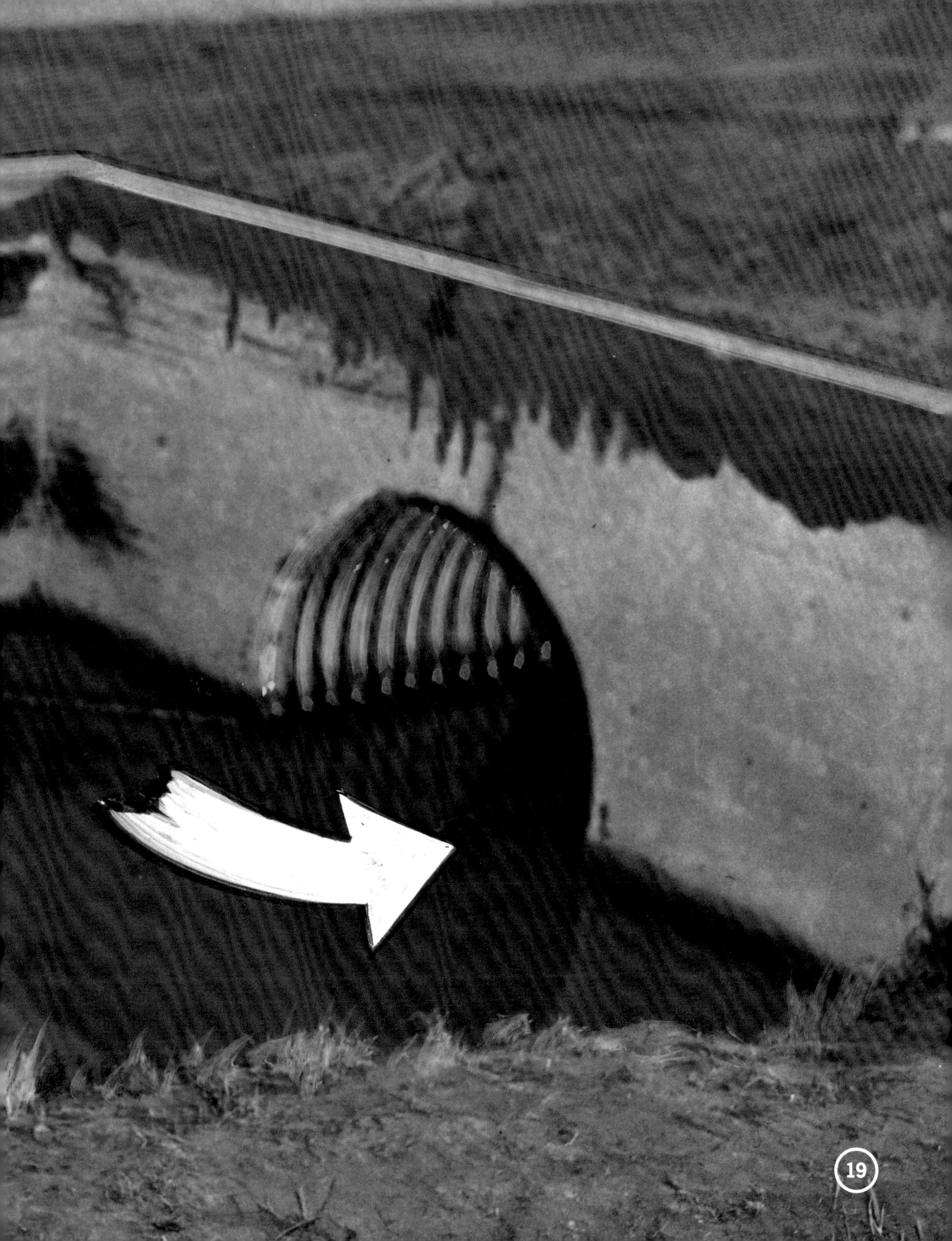

RE

ENACTMENTS

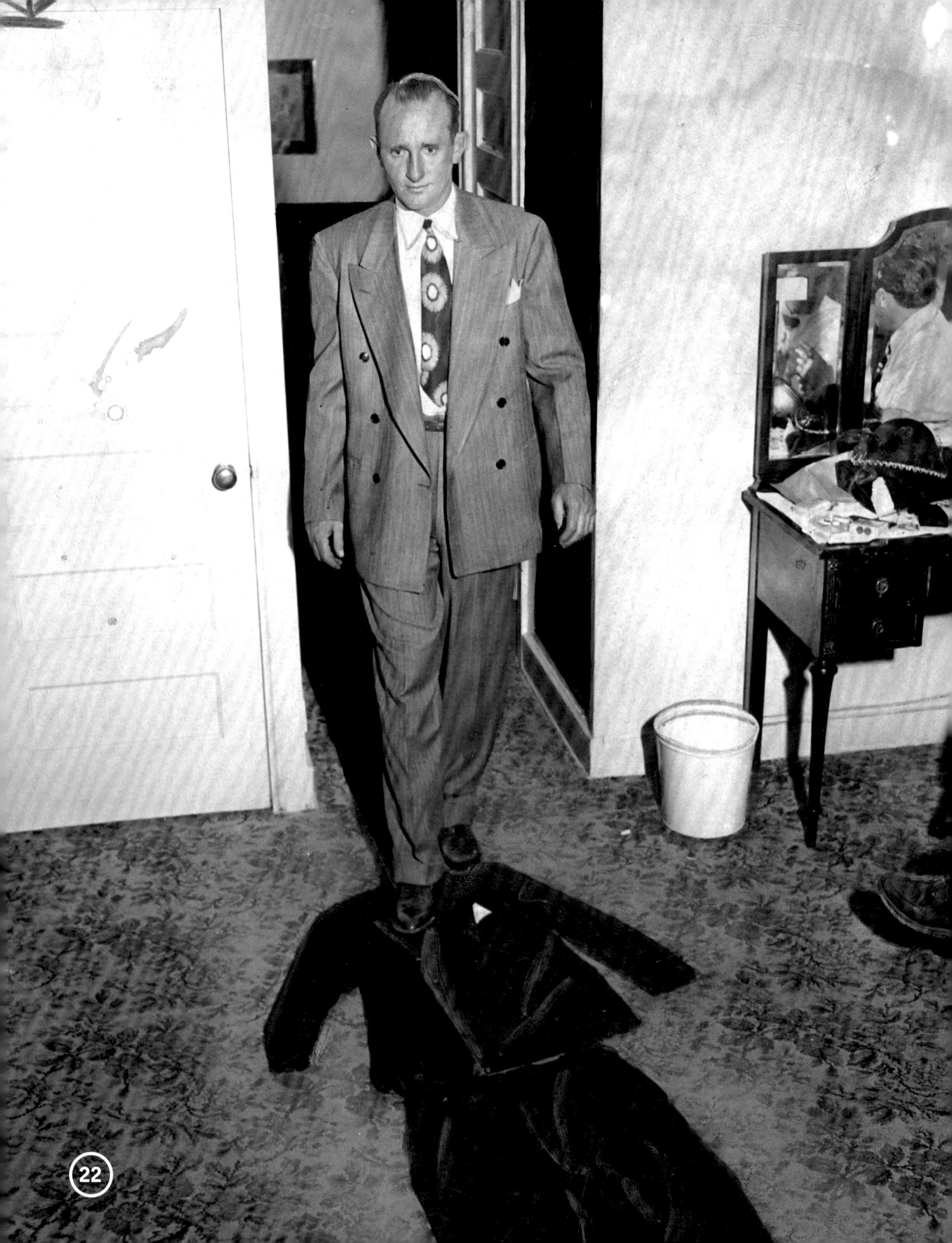

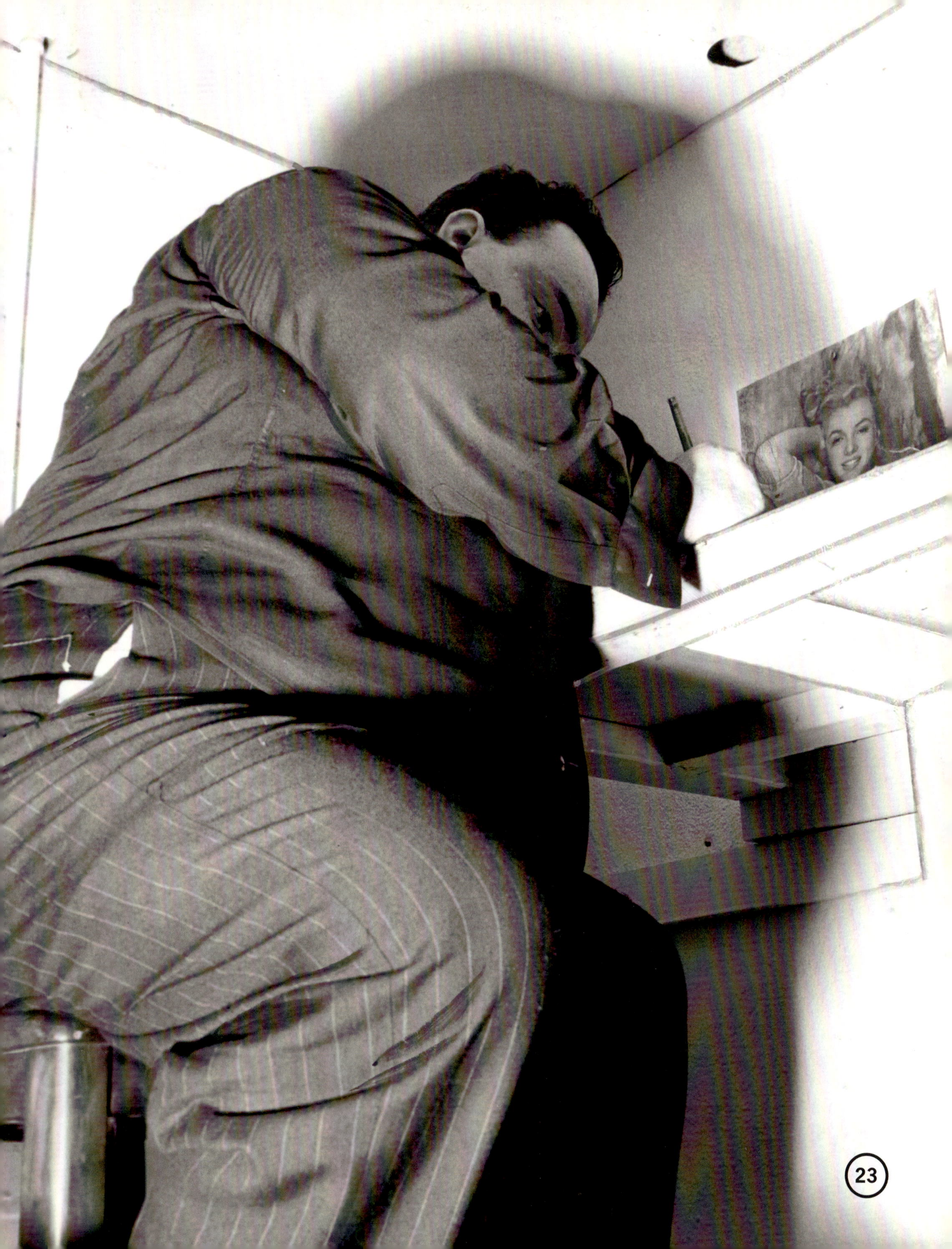

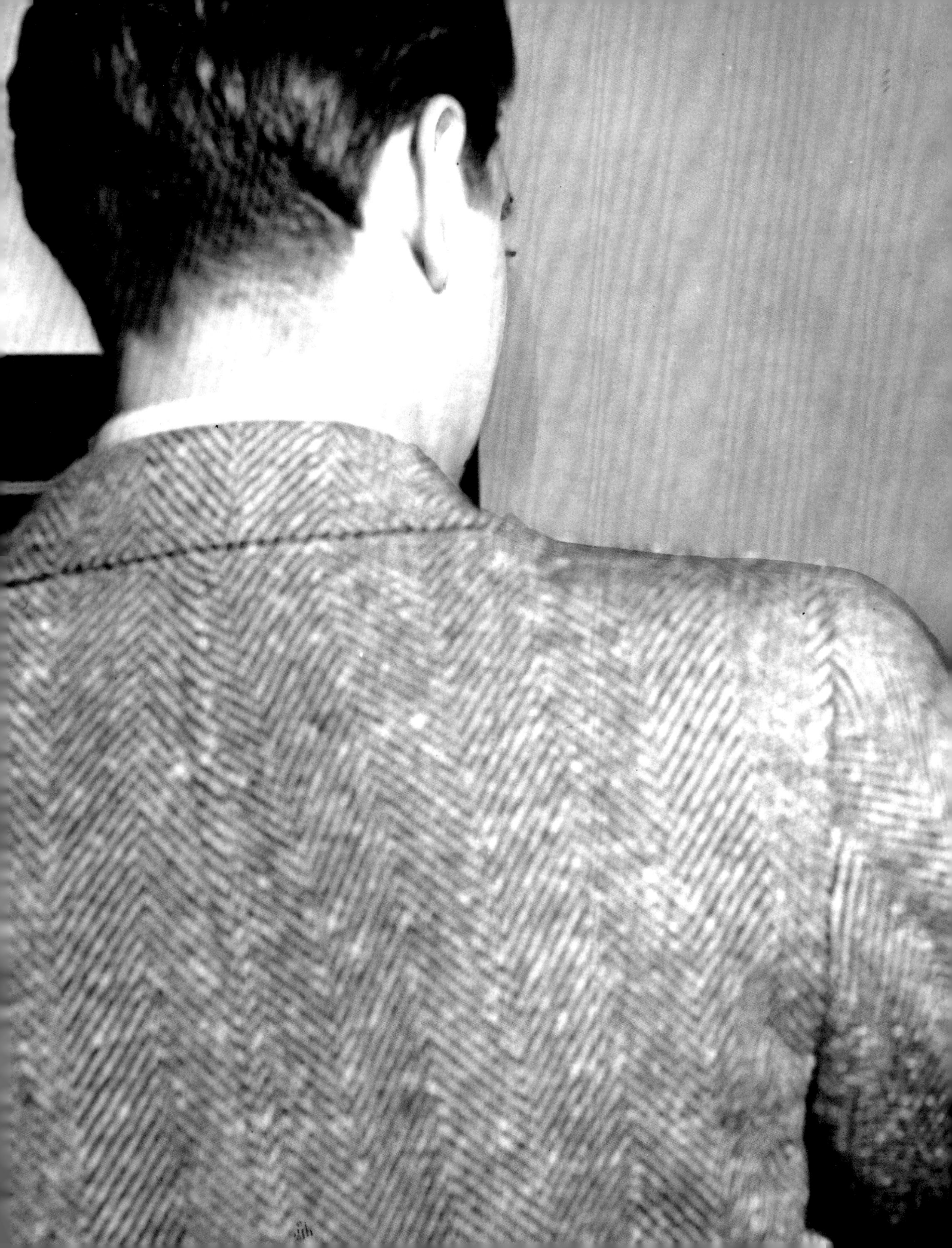

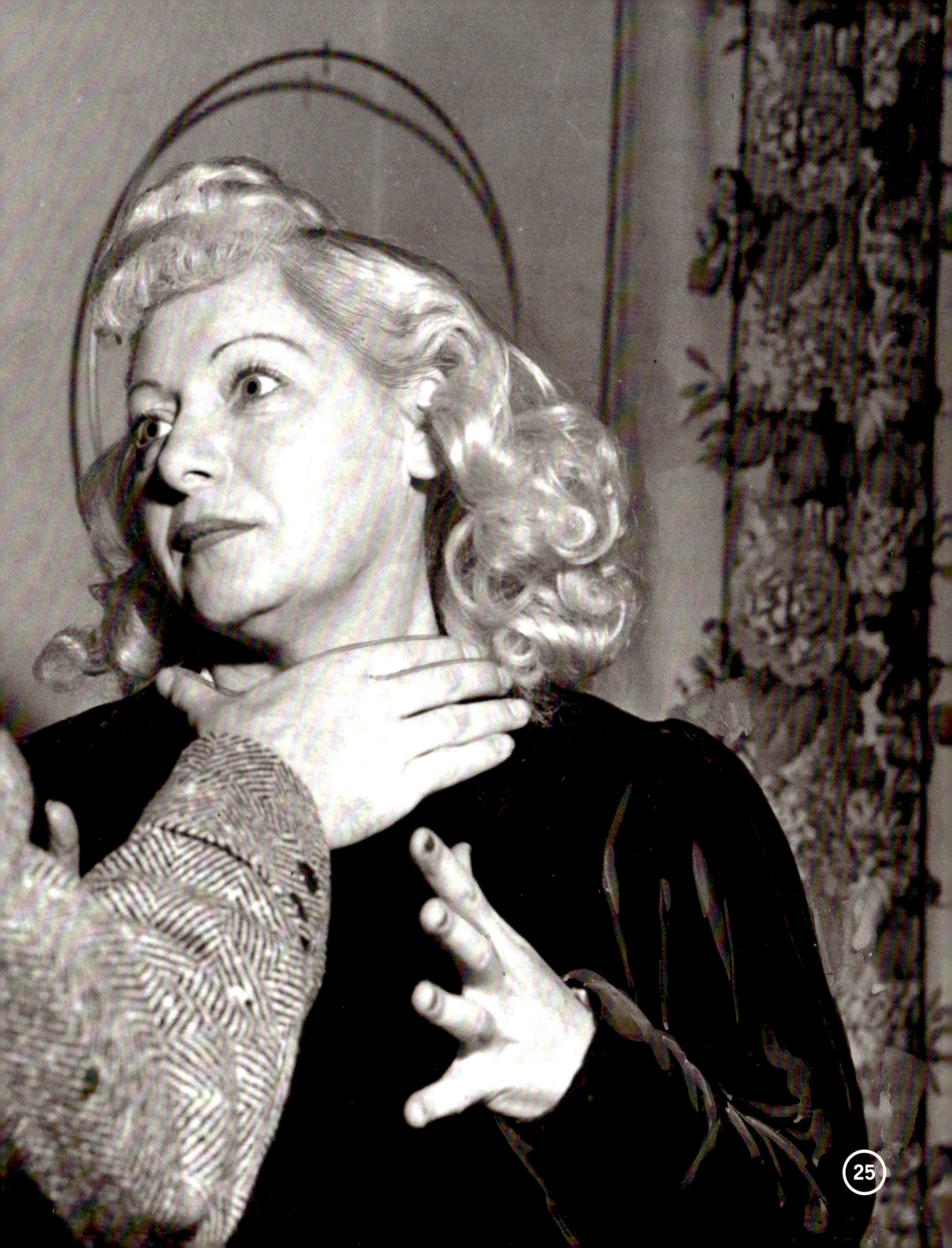

25

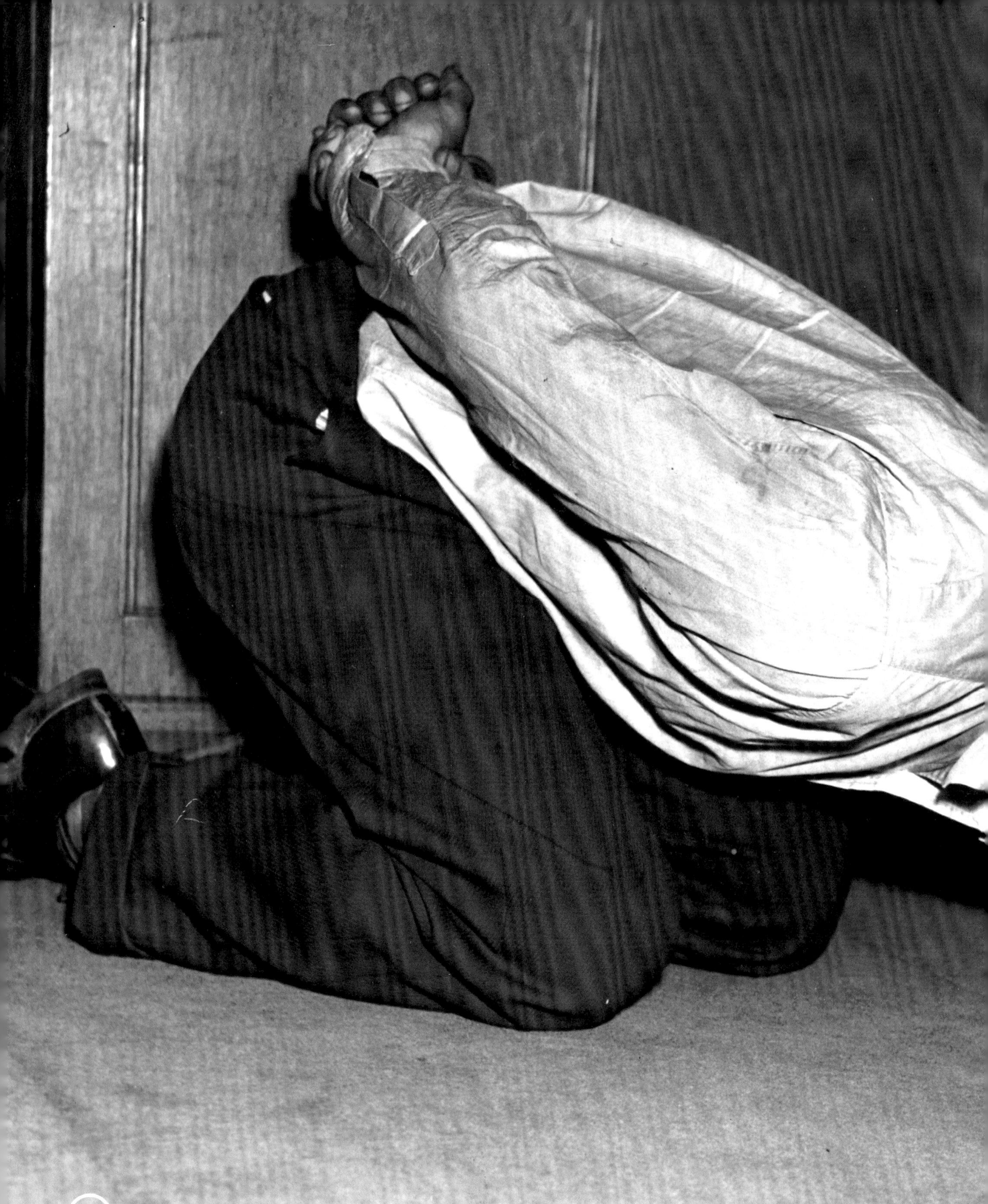

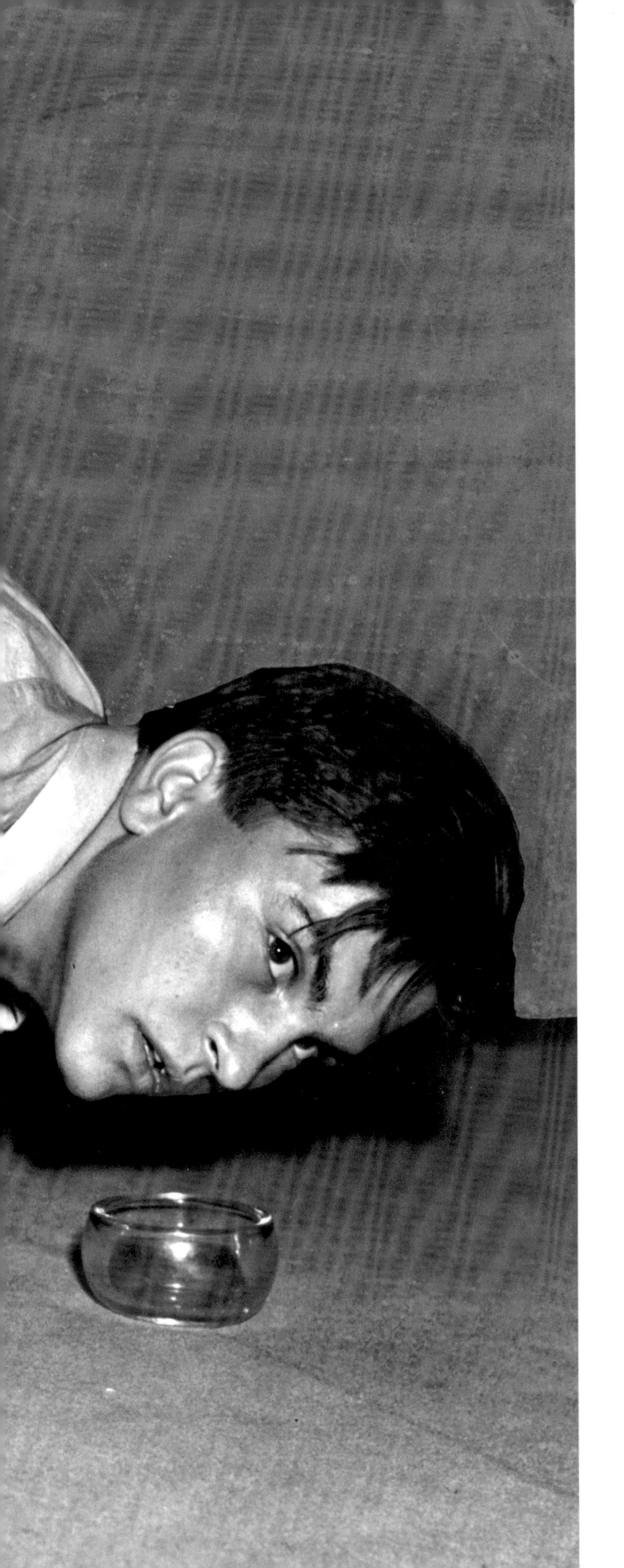

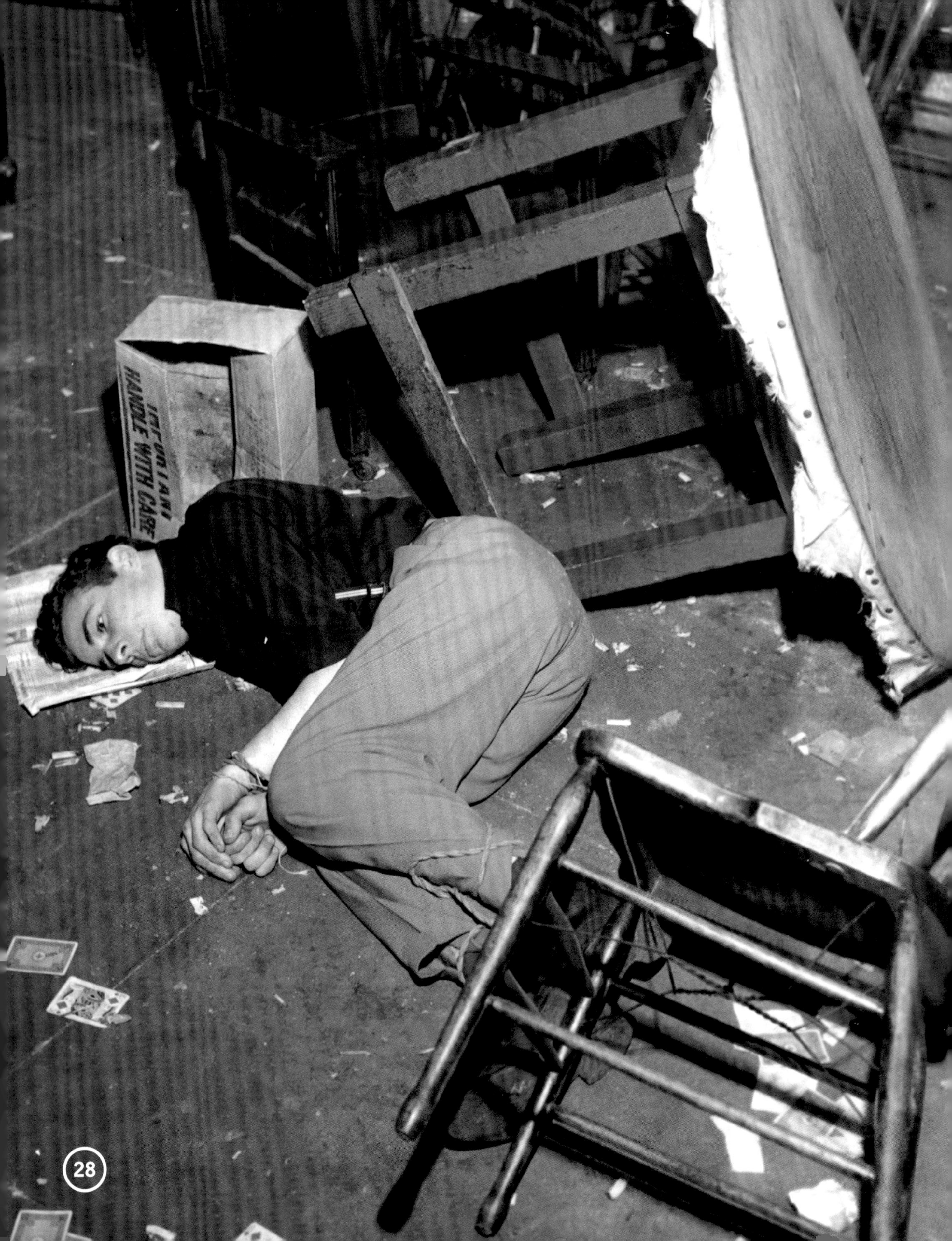
IMPORTANT
HANDLE WITH CARE

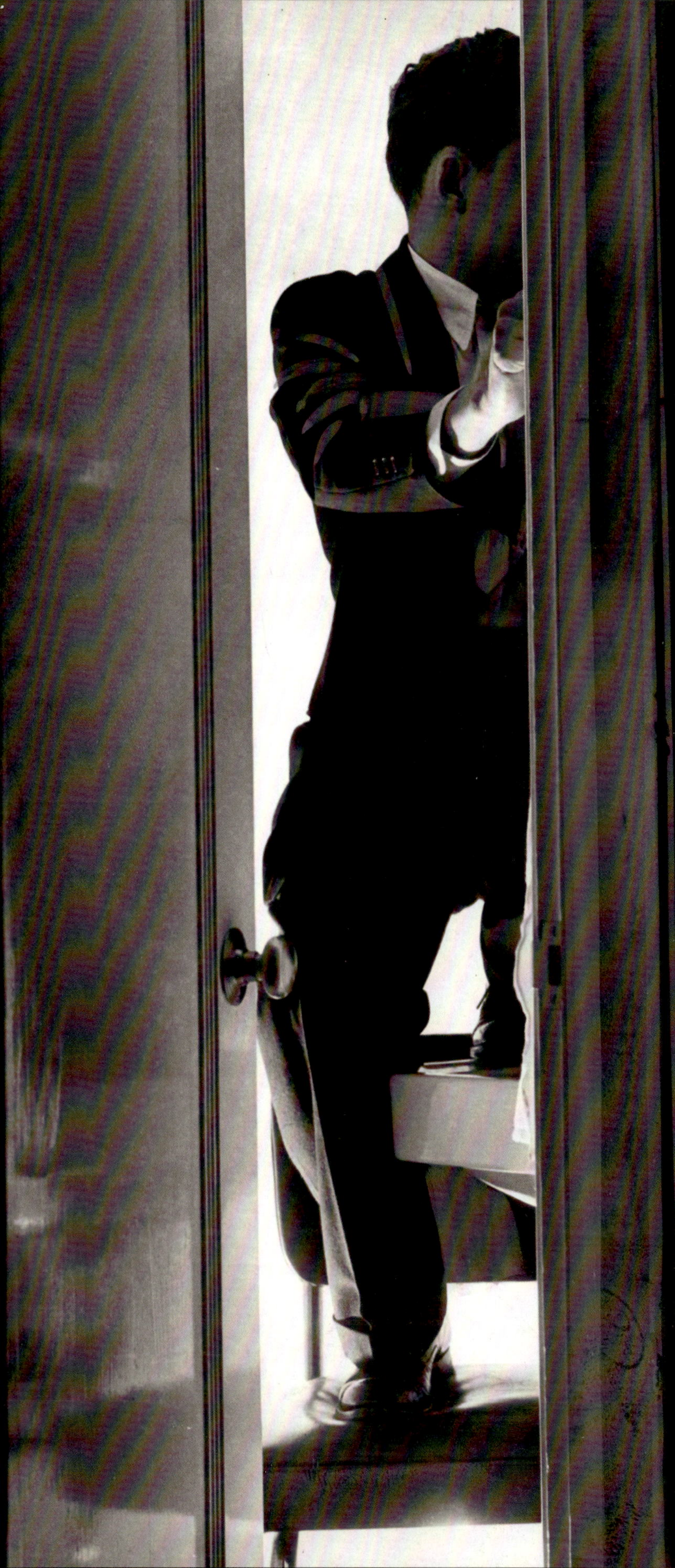

EVIDENCE

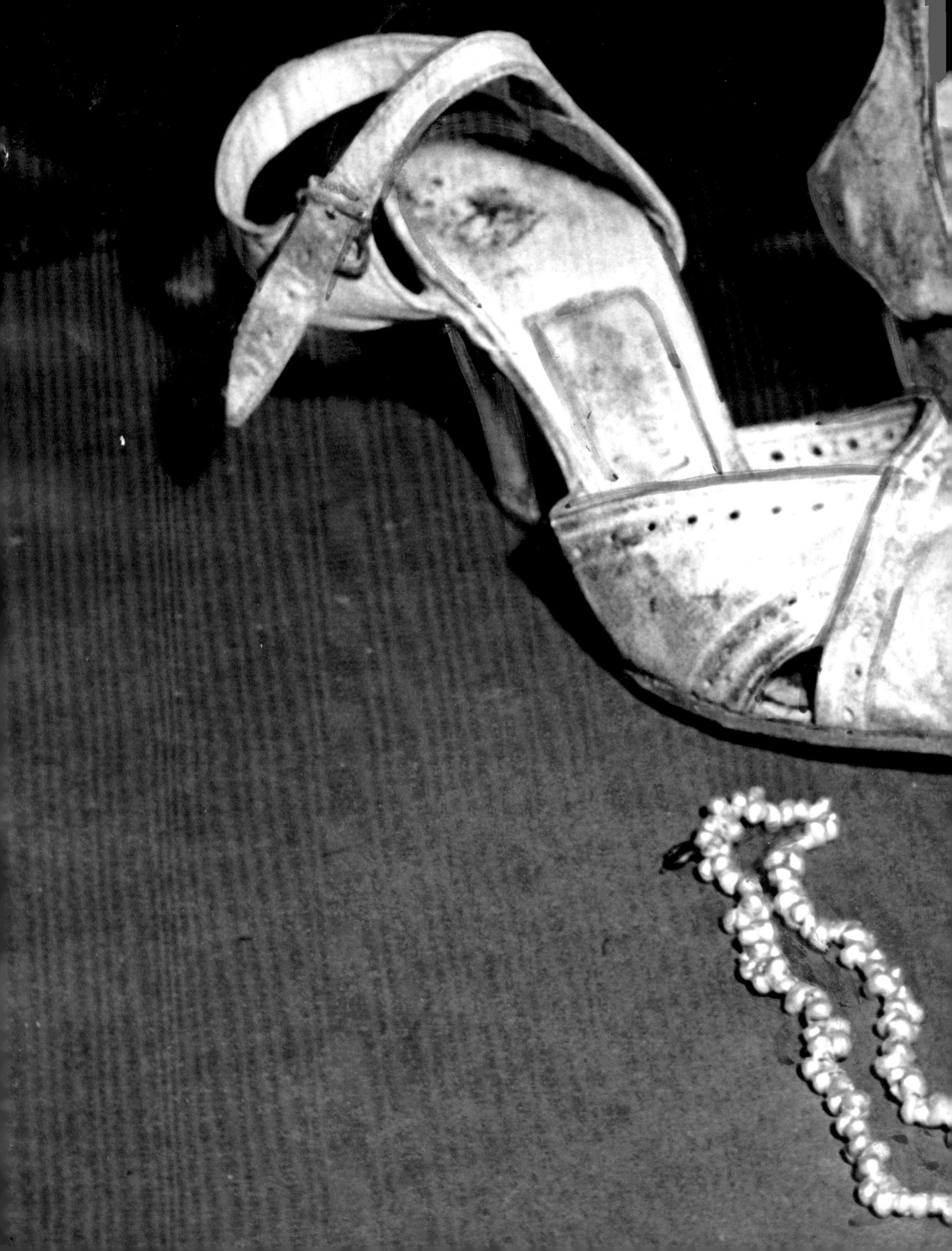

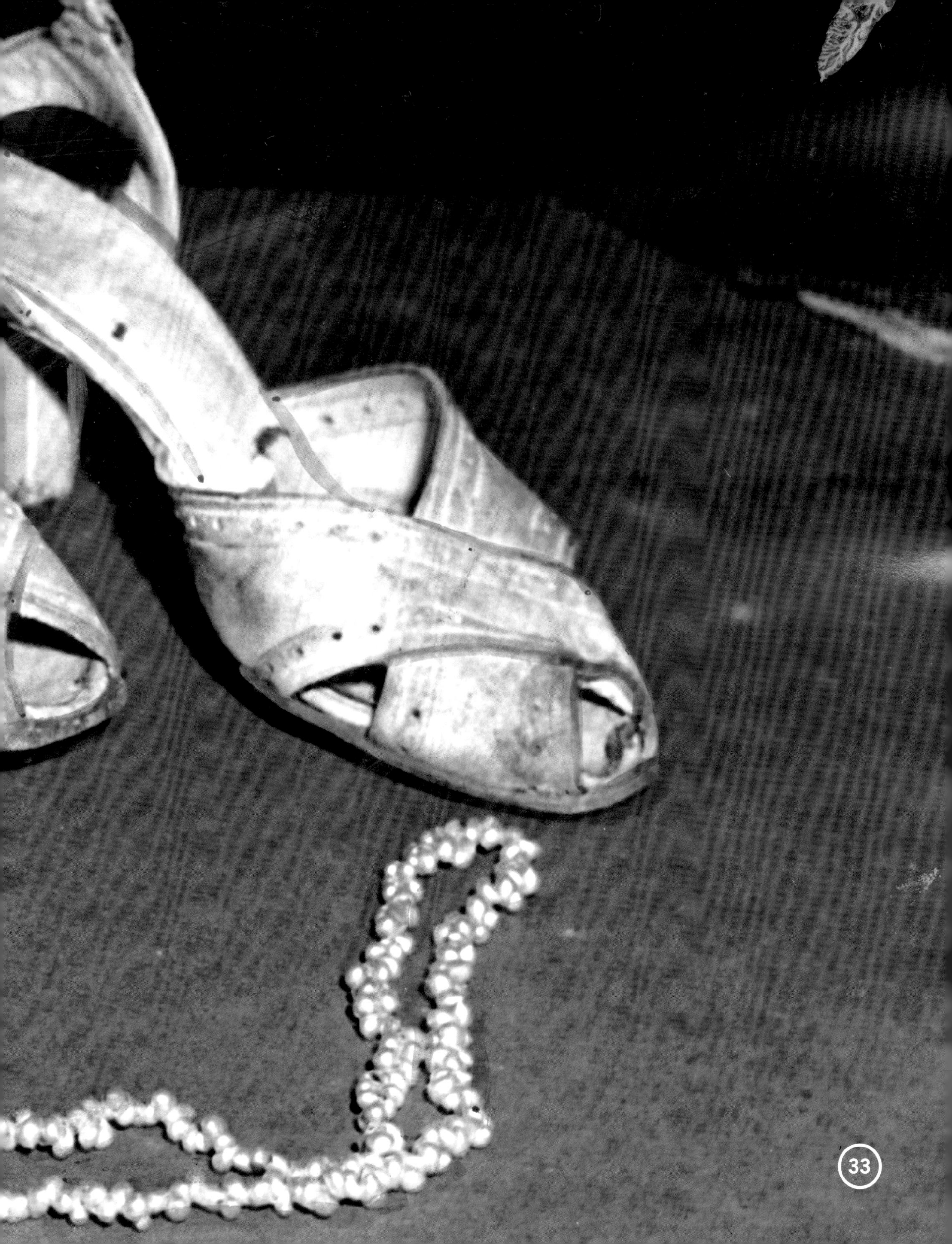

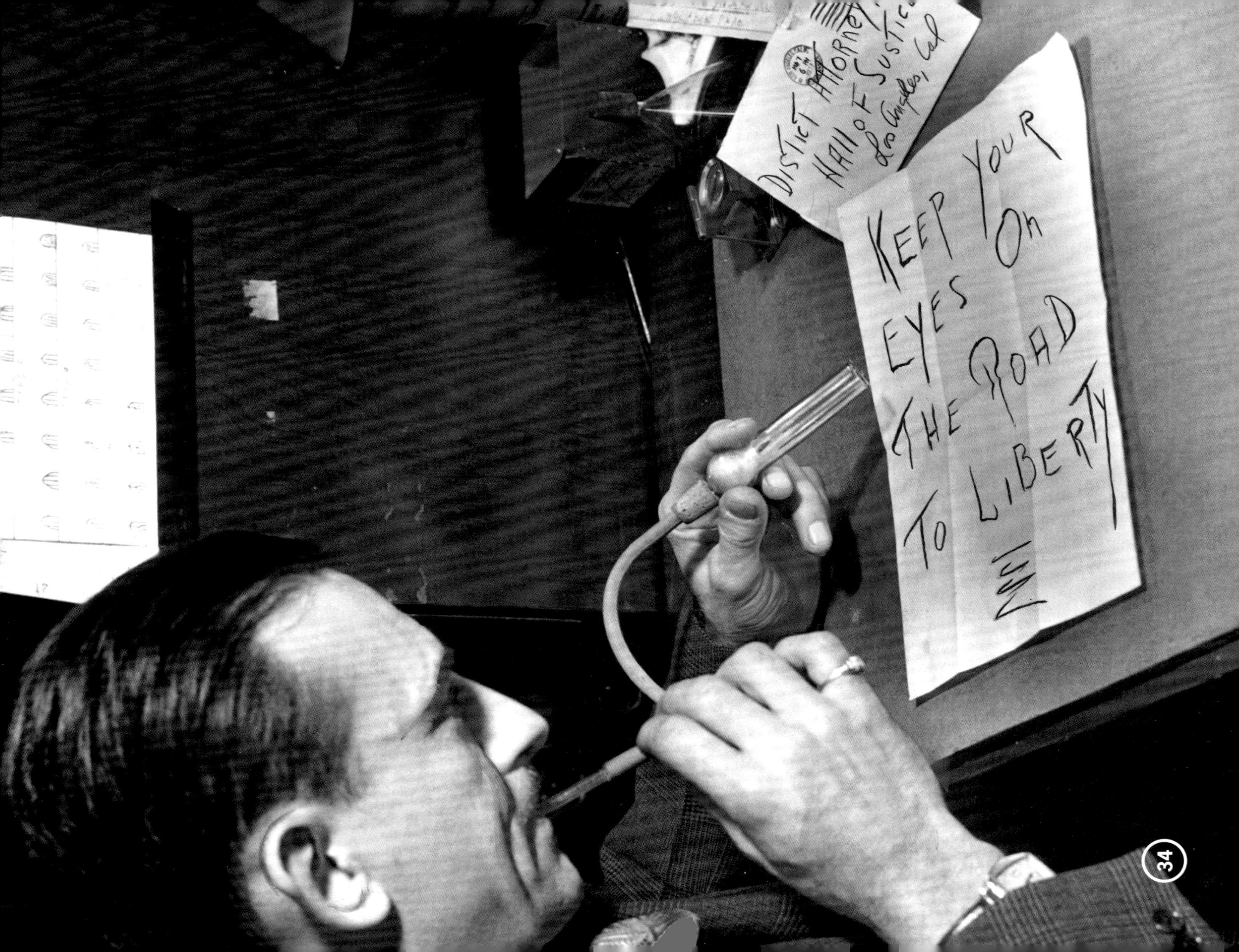

KEEP YOUR
EYES ON
THE ROAD
TO LIBERTY

DISTICT Attorney
HAll OF SUSTICE
Los Angeles, Cal

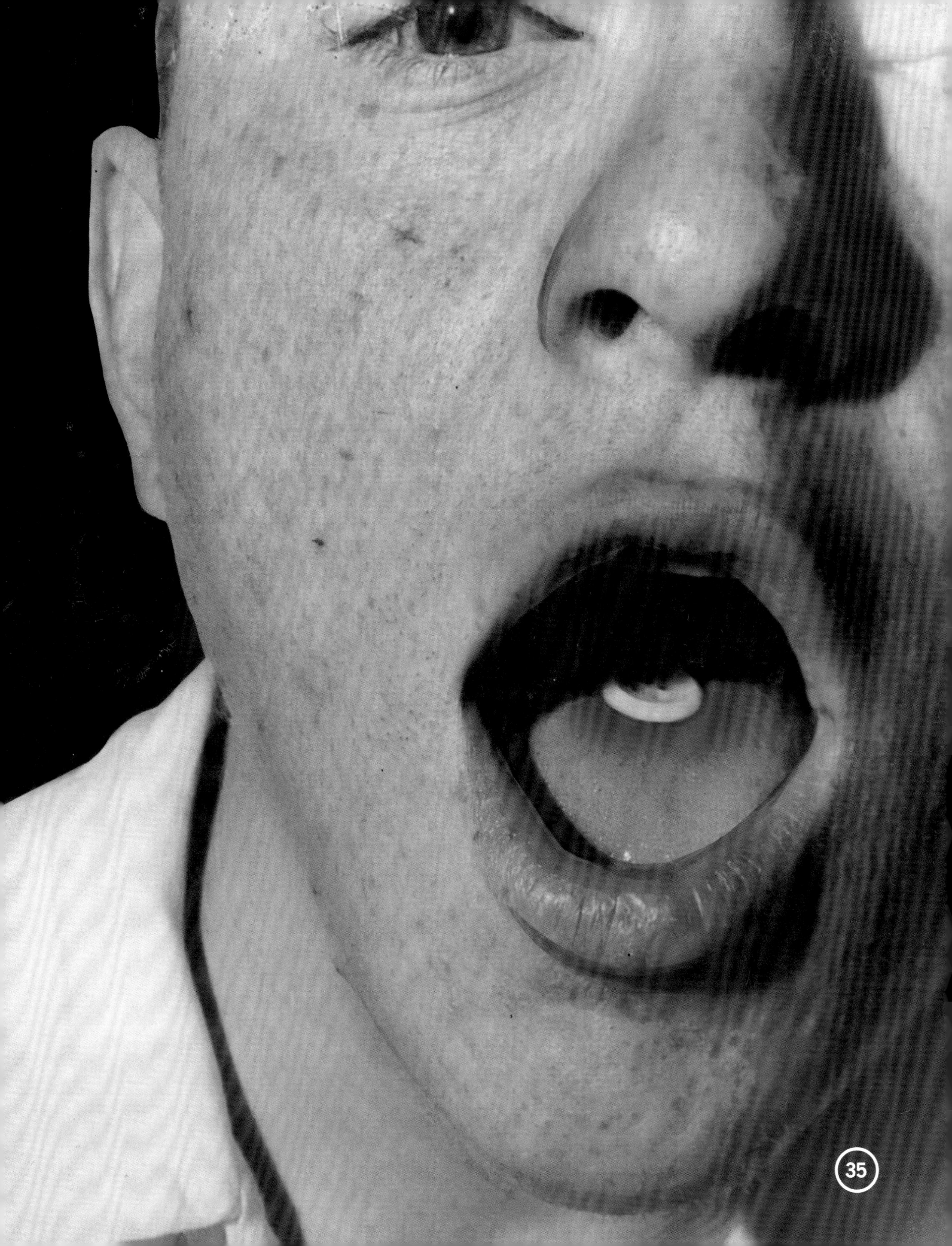

CHILD

CUSTODY

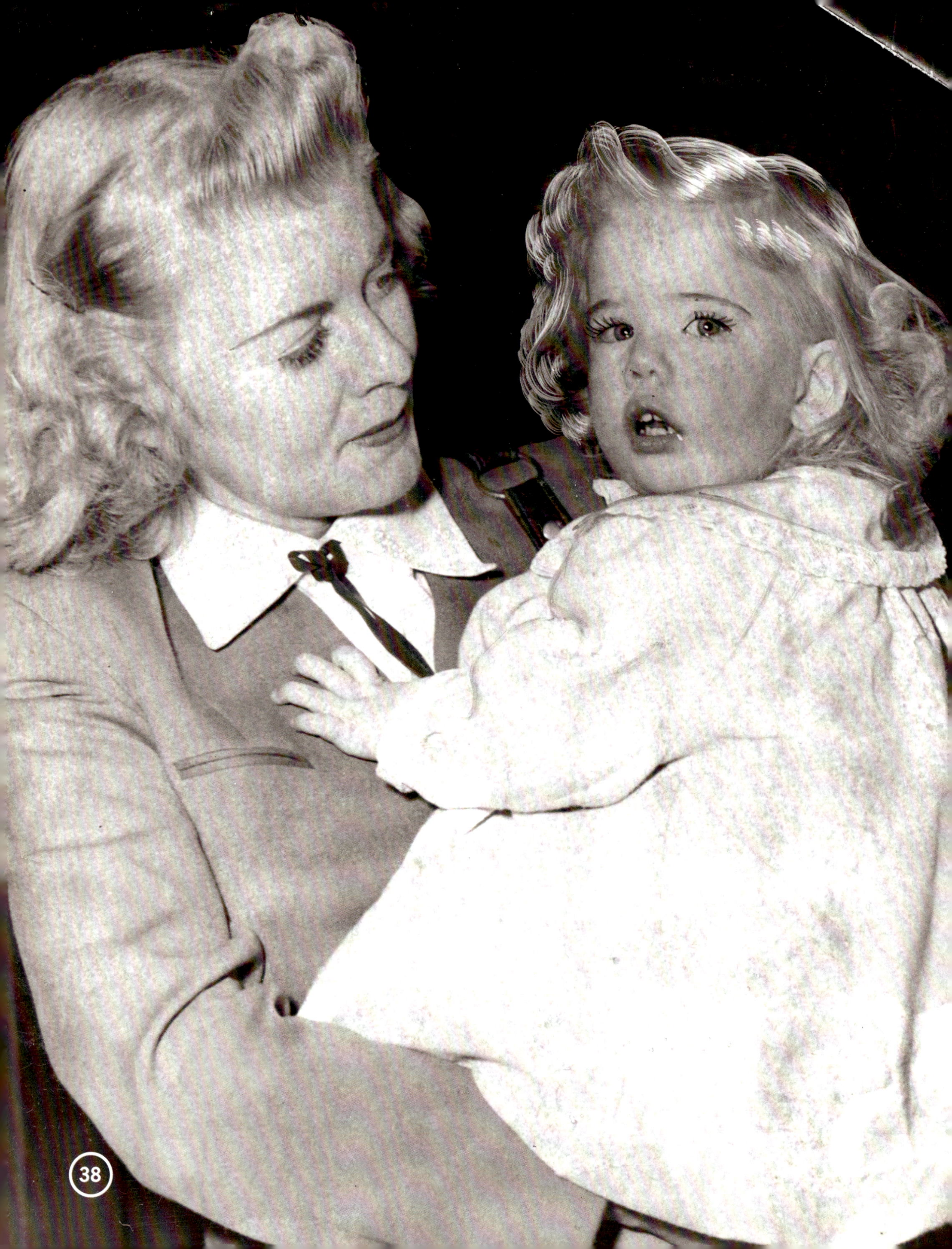

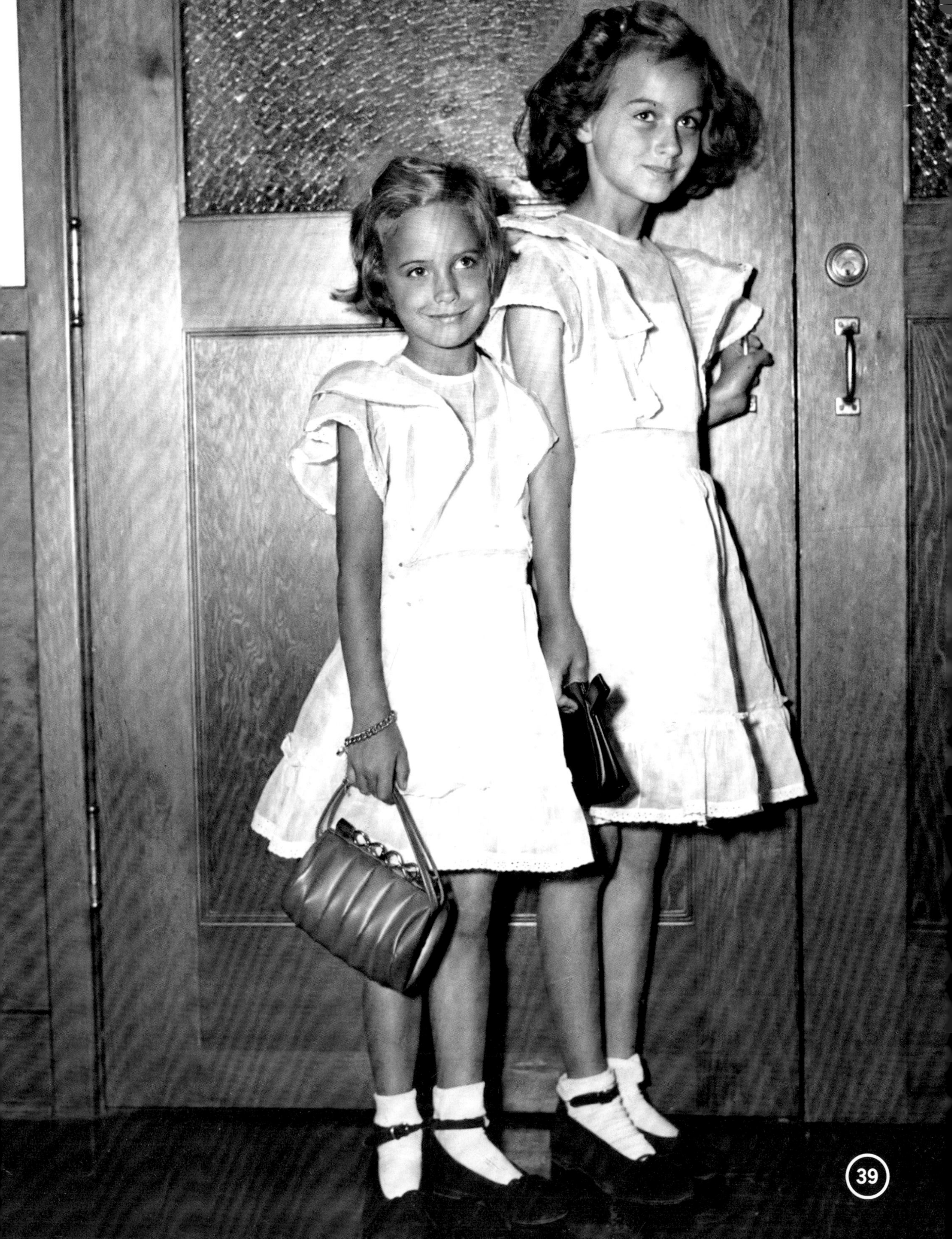

39

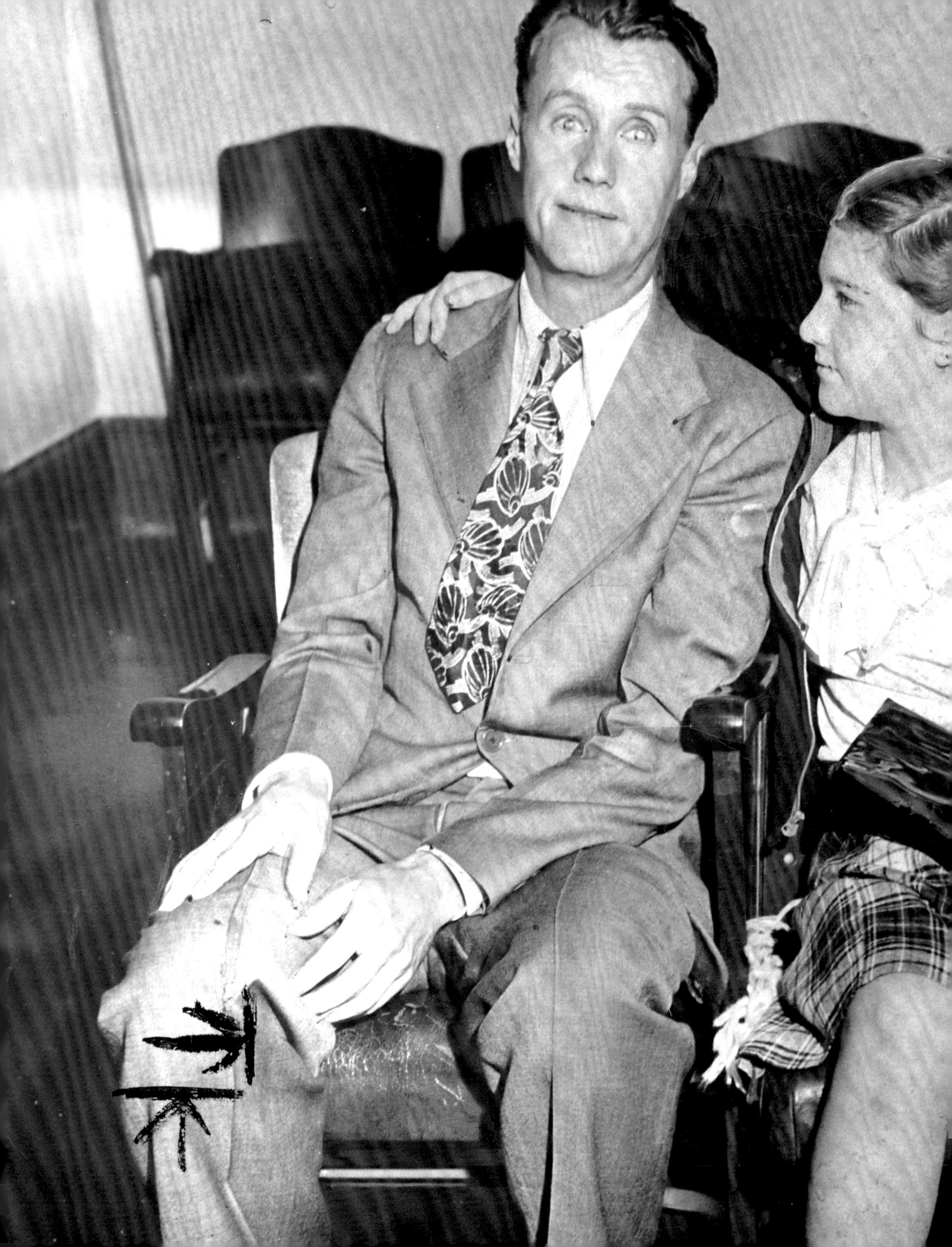

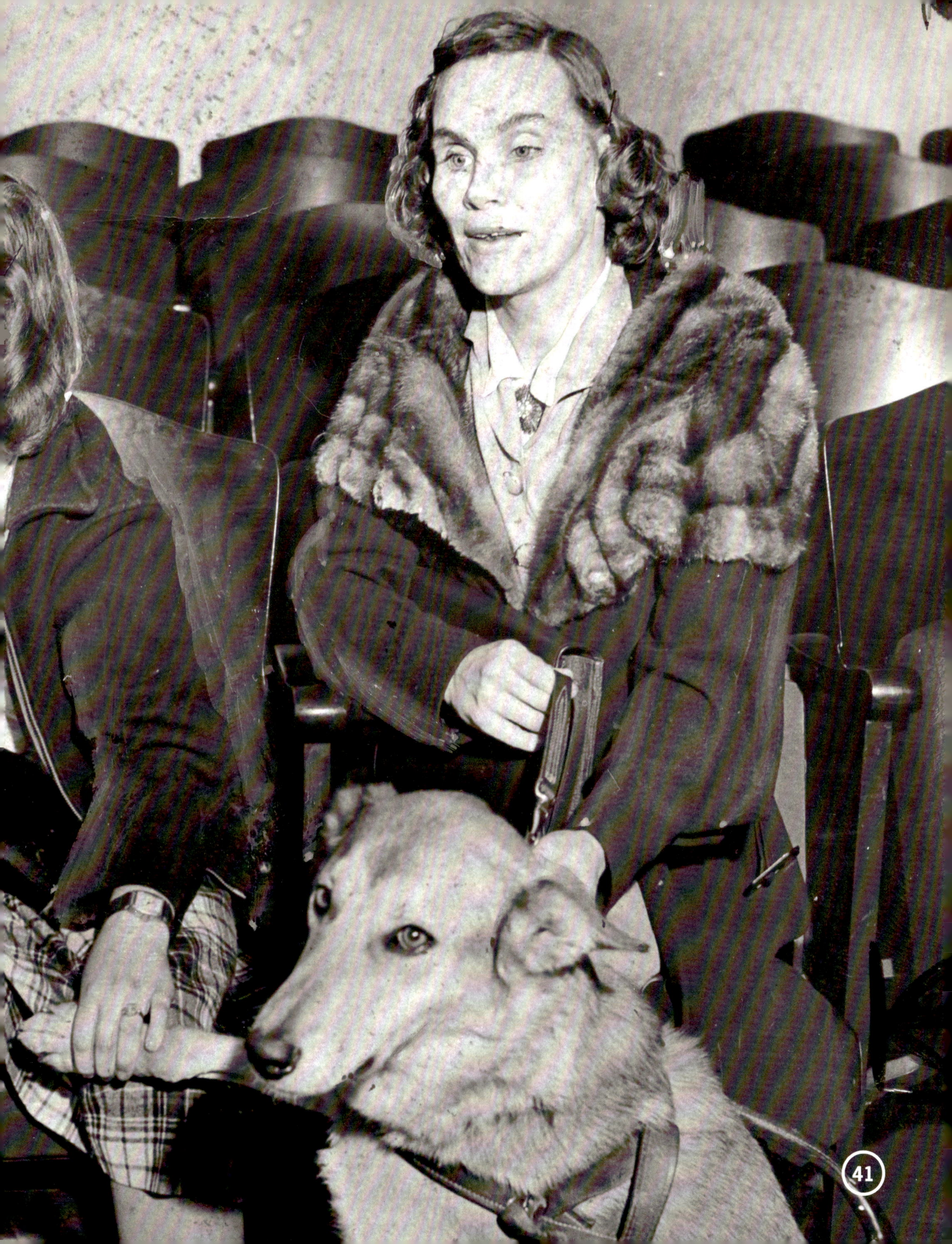

VICTIMS

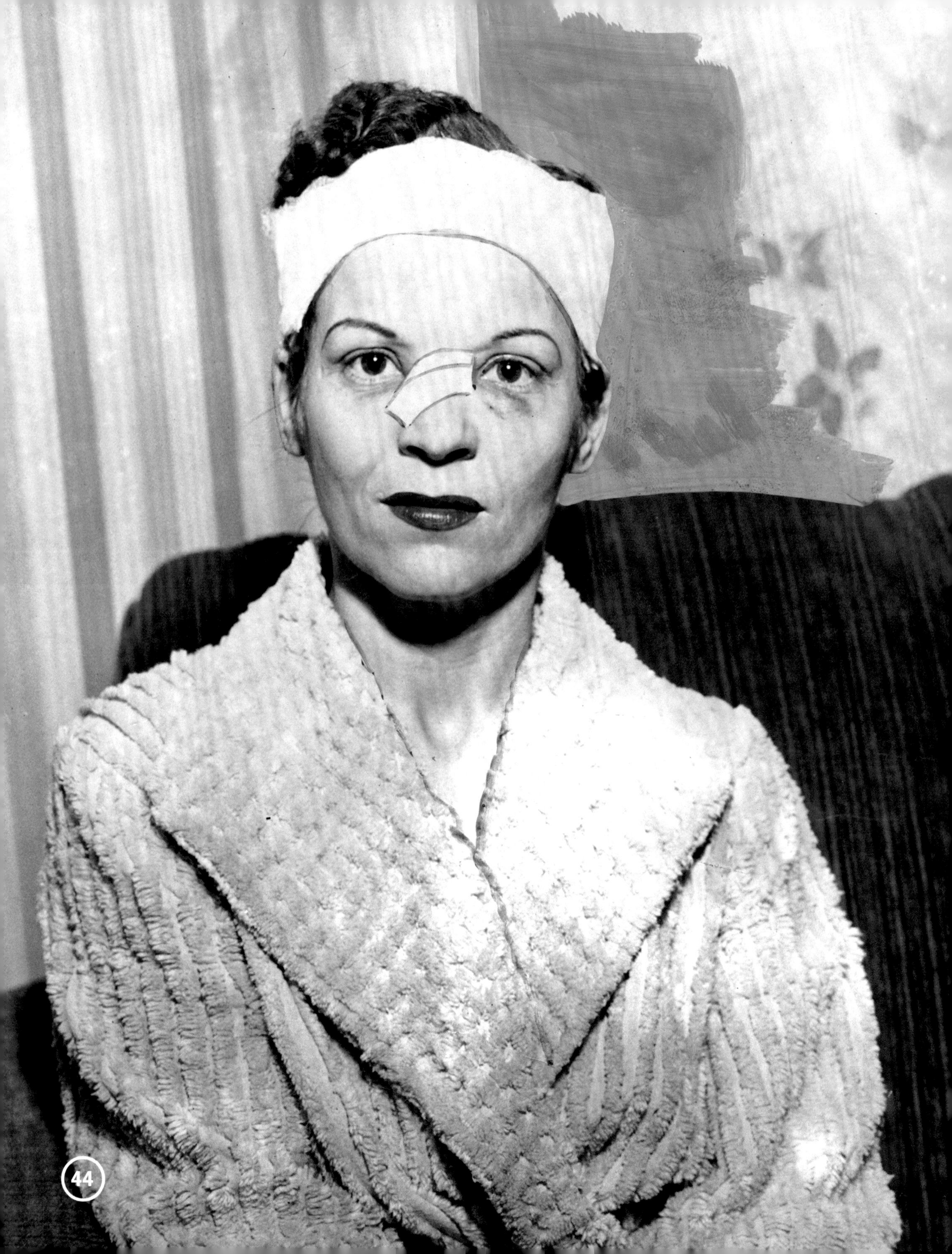

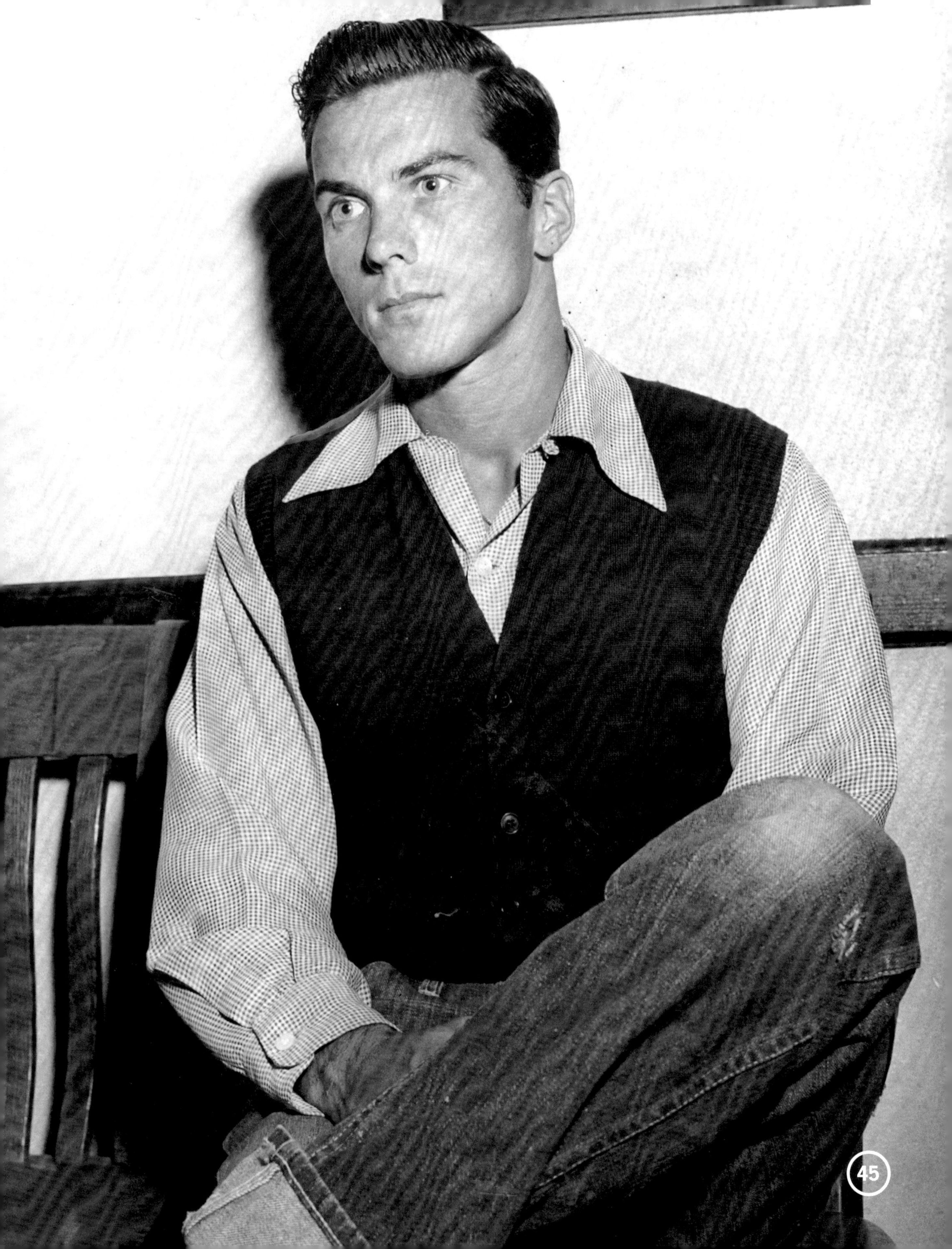

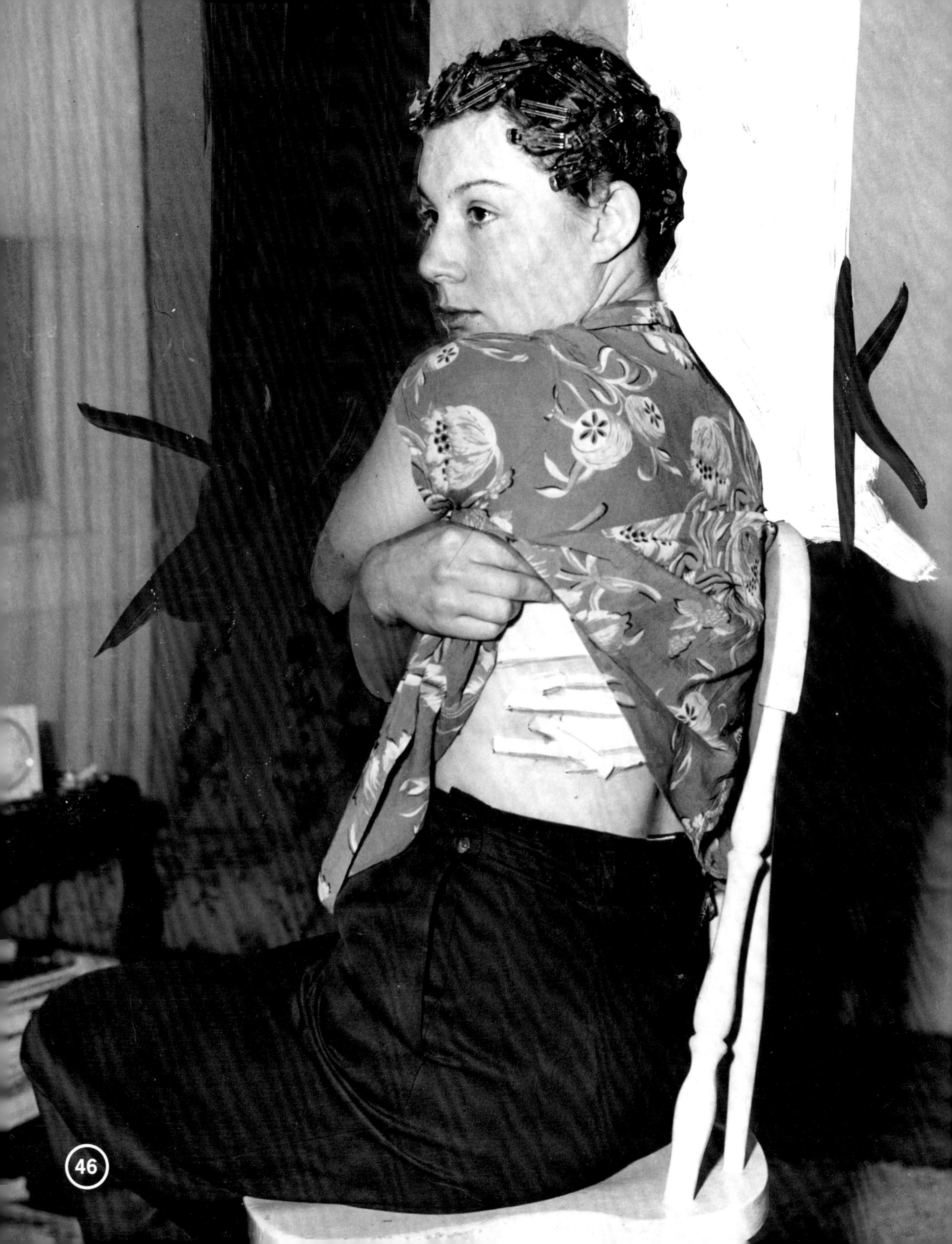

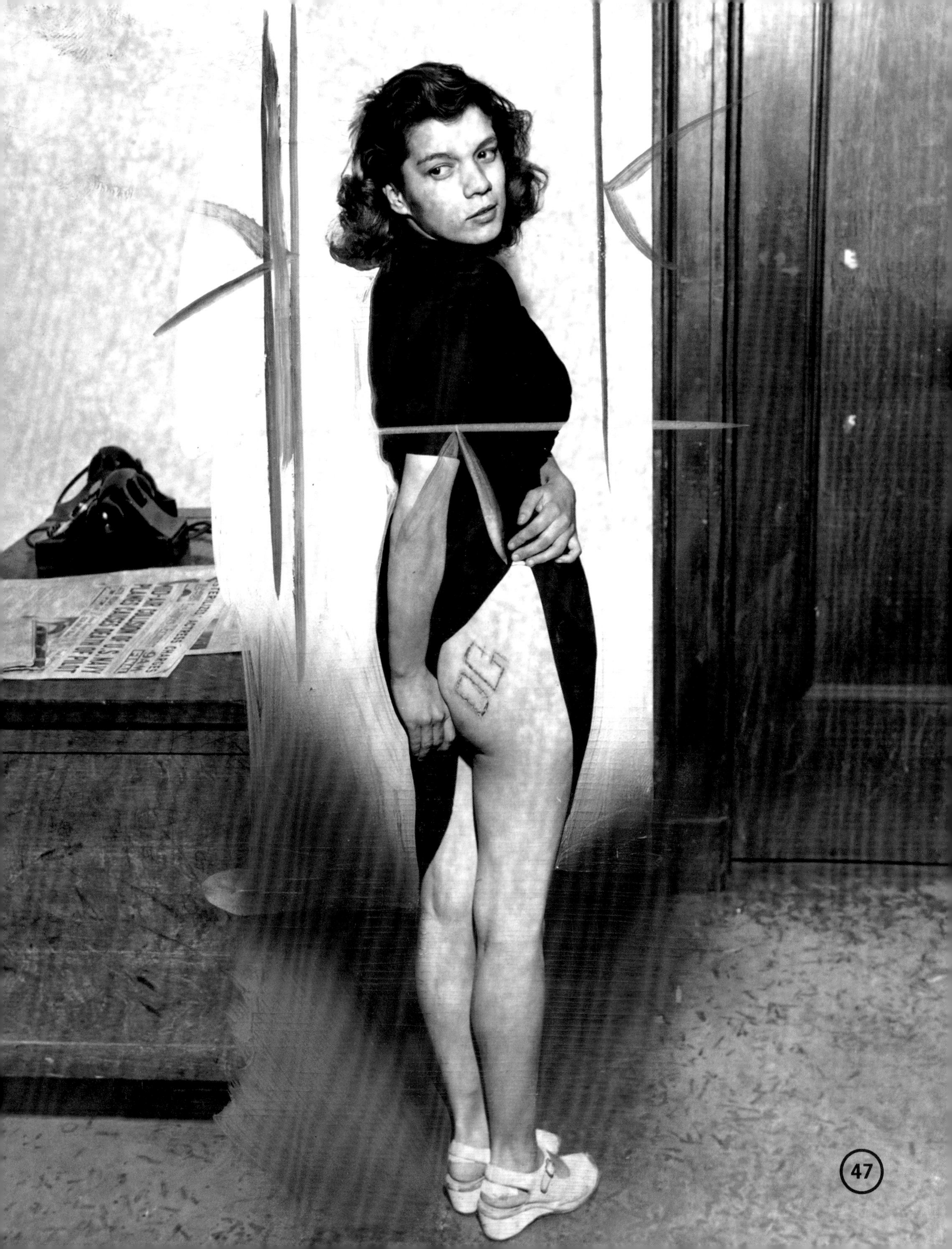

DOPE RAIDS

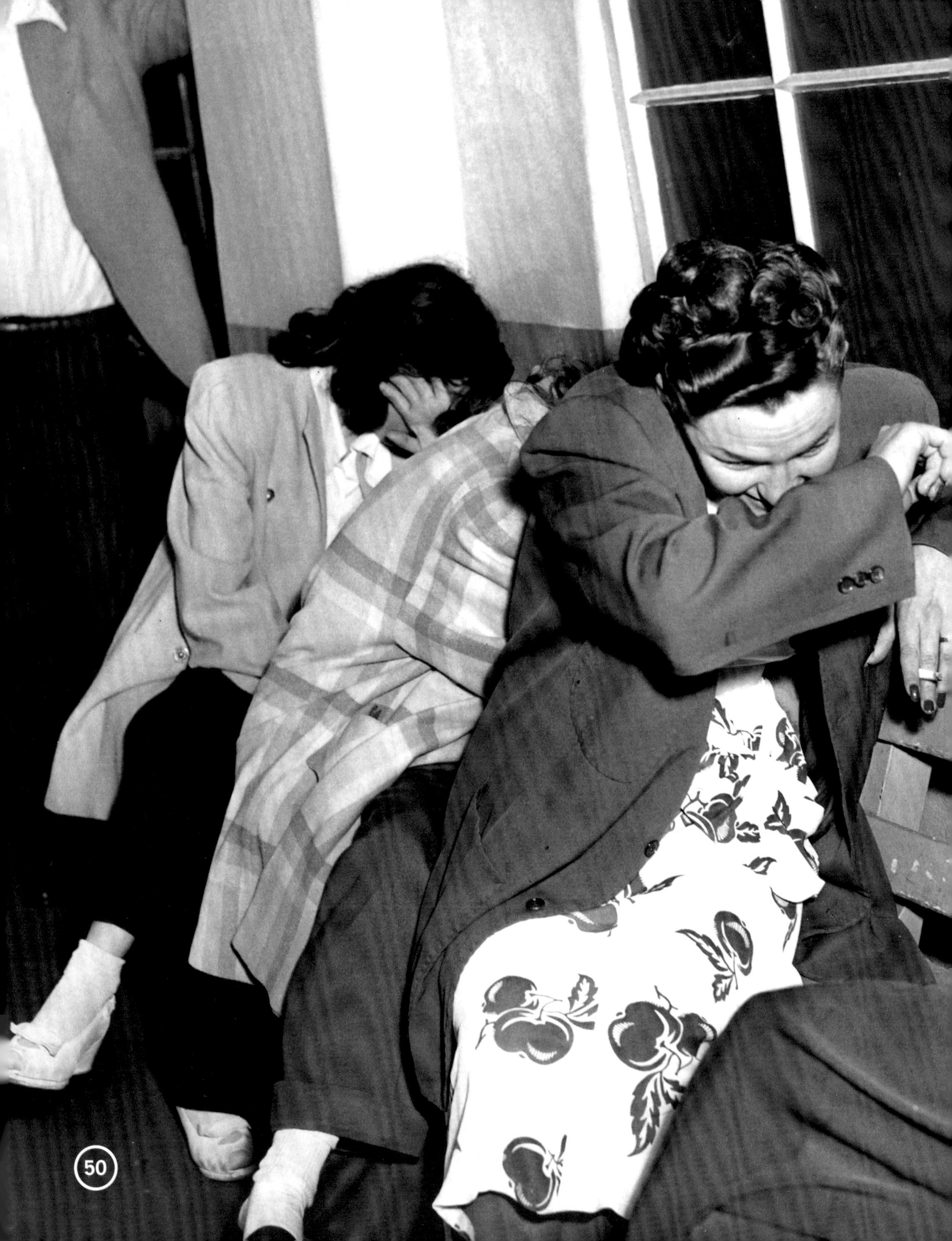

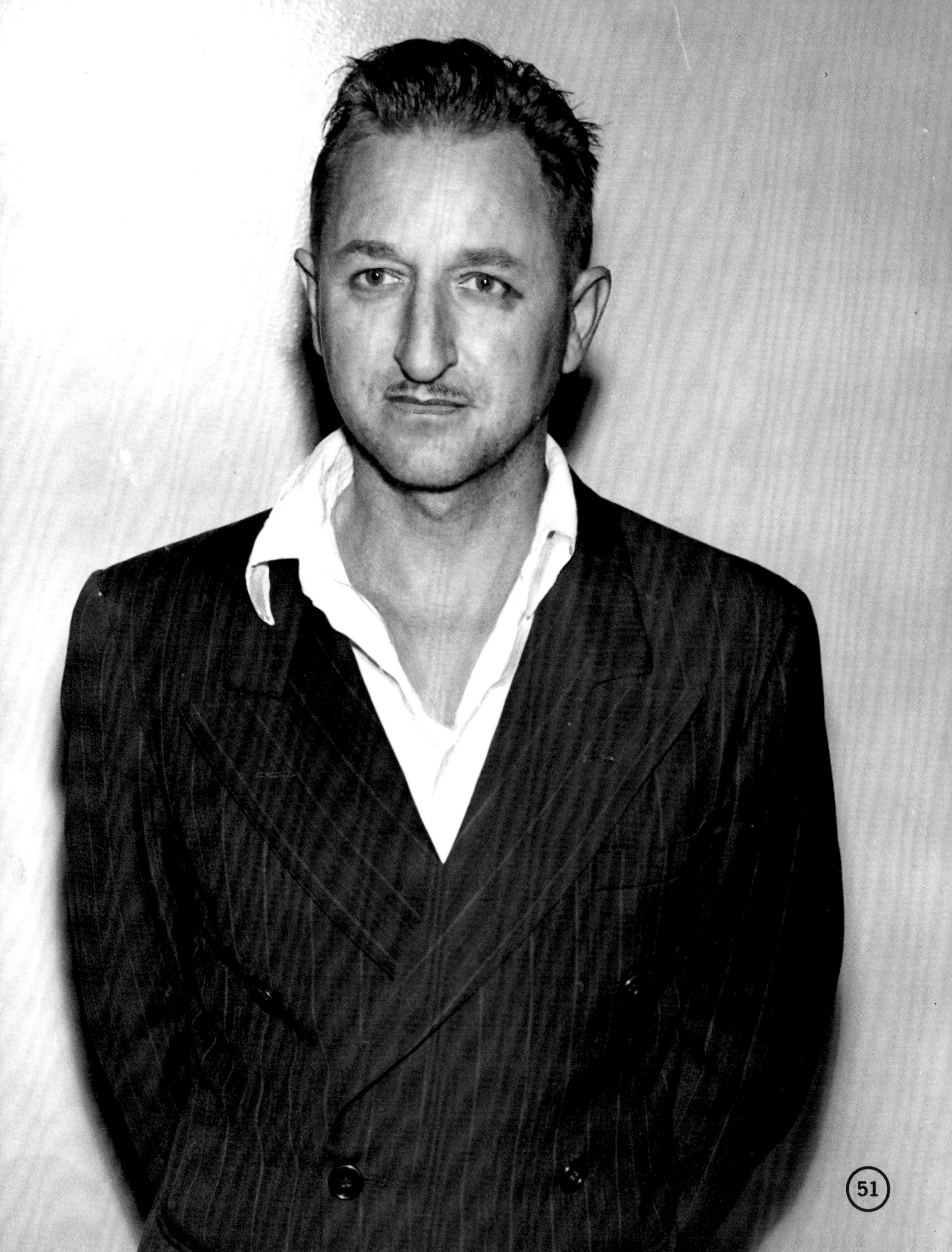

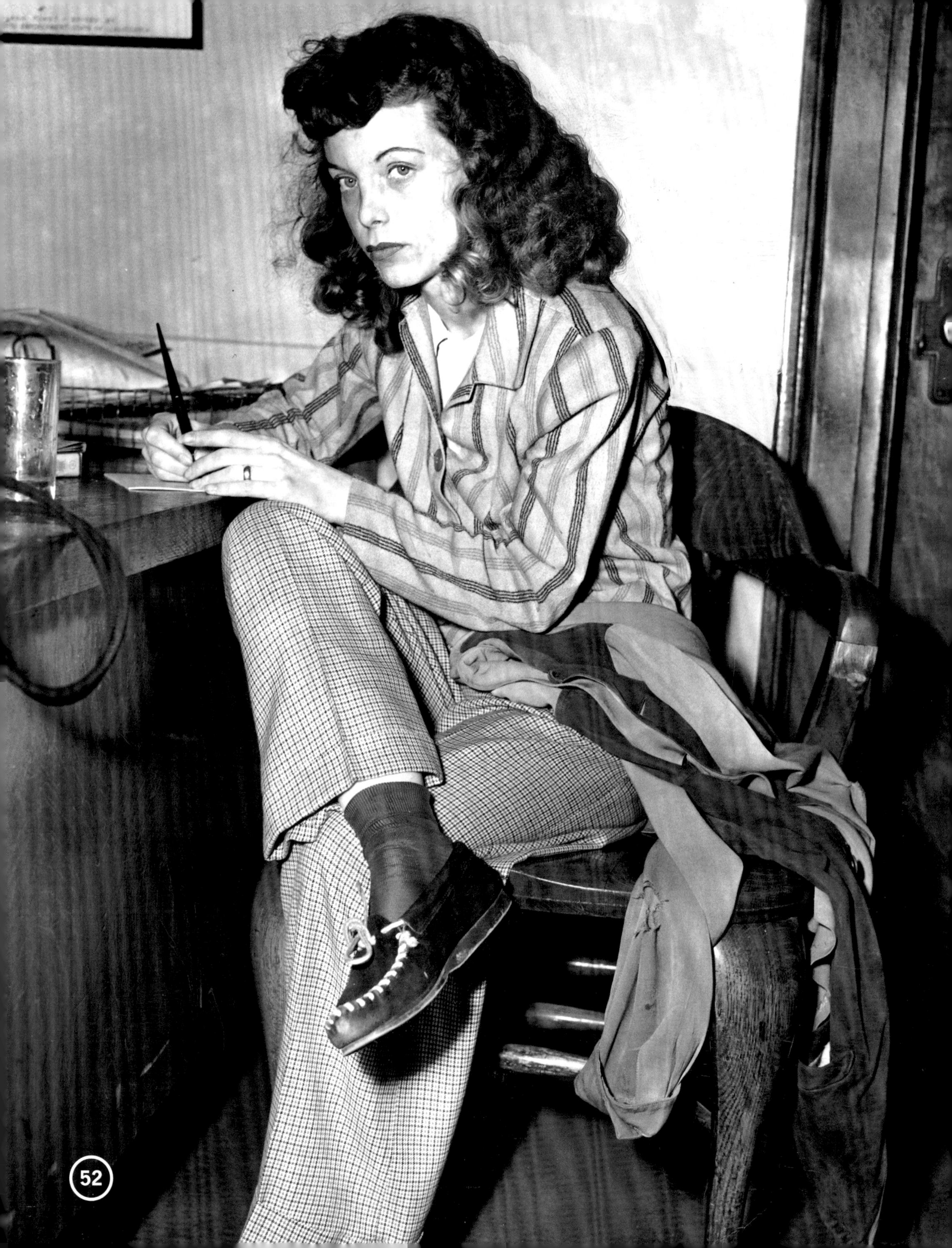

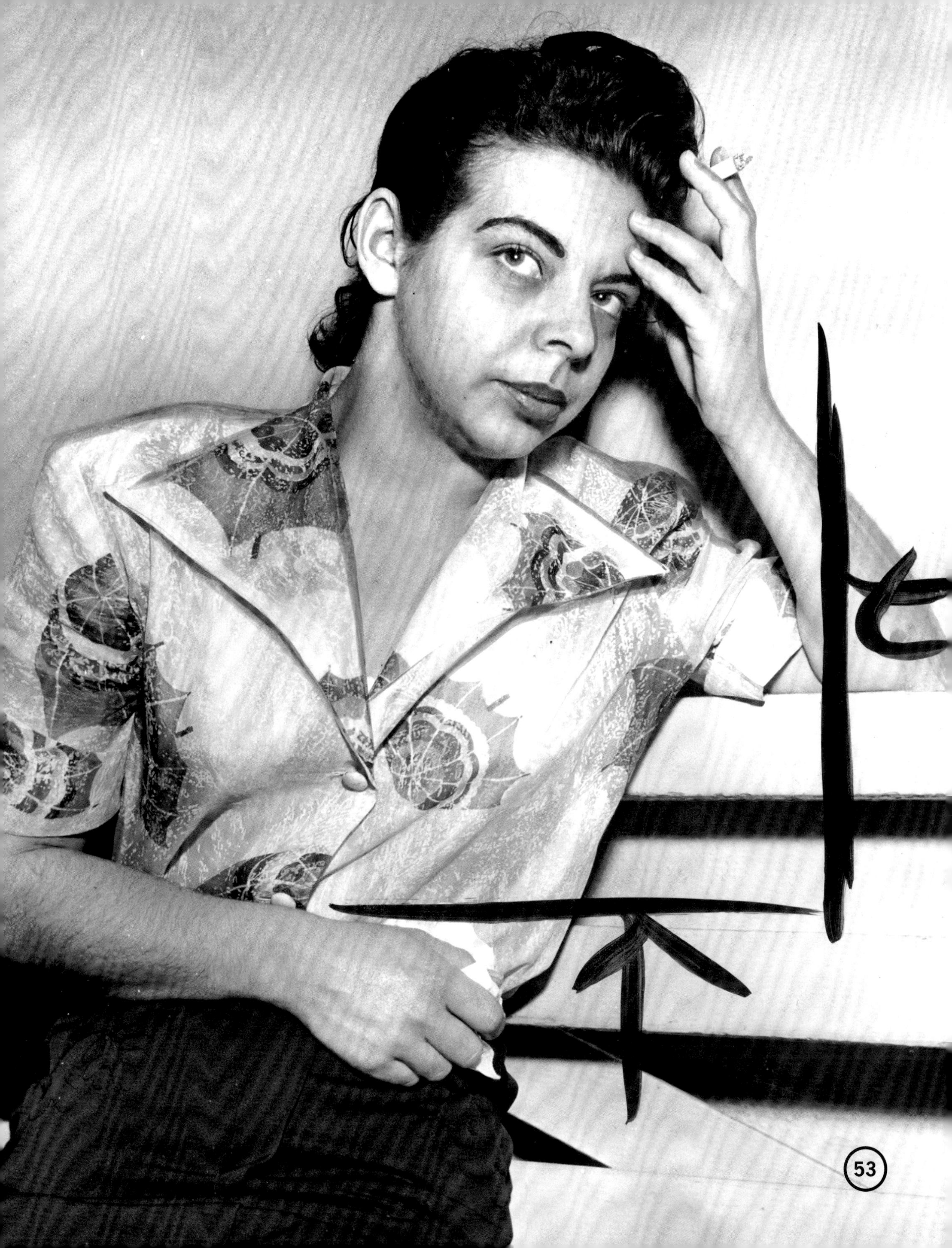

HOLD-UP

SUSPECTS

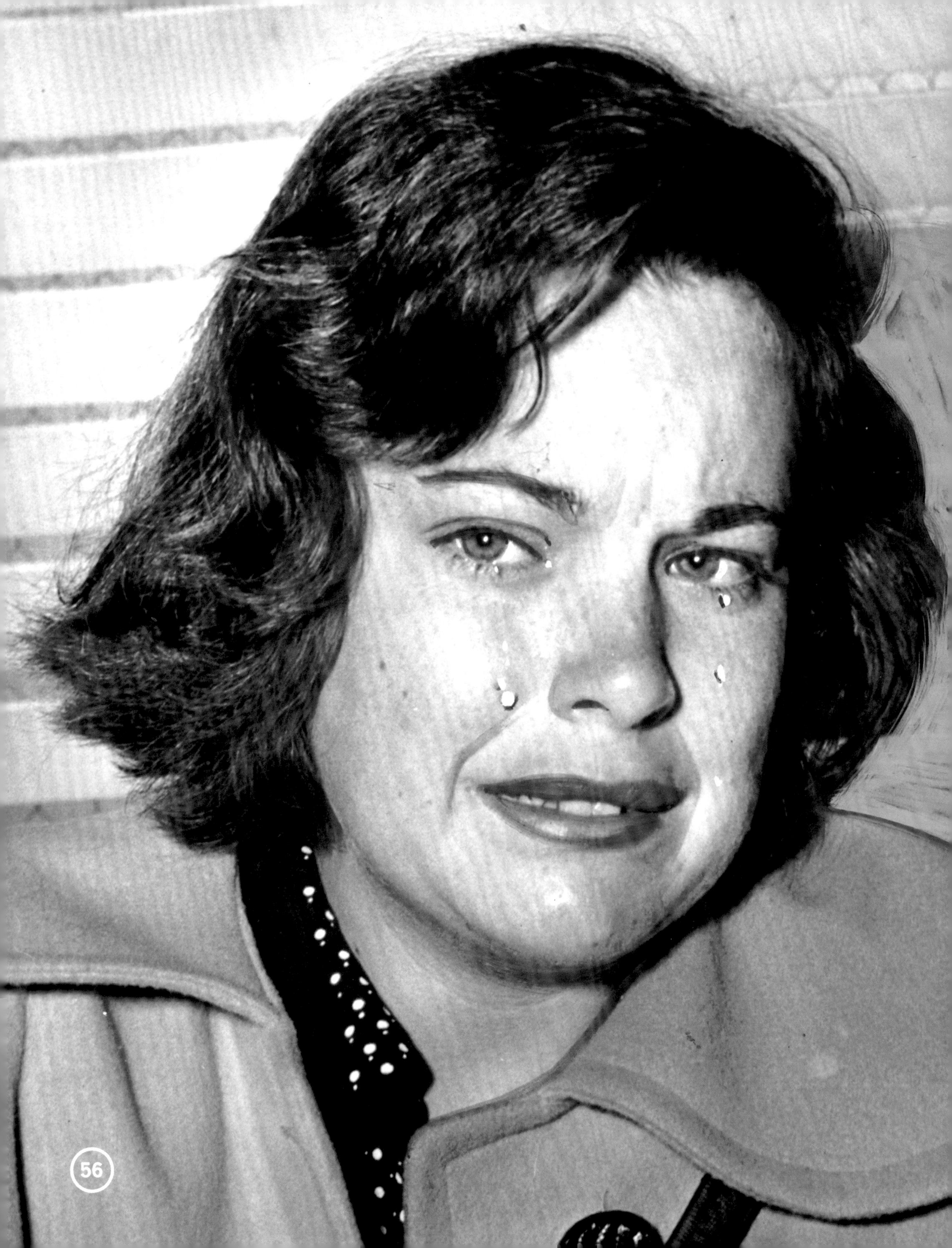

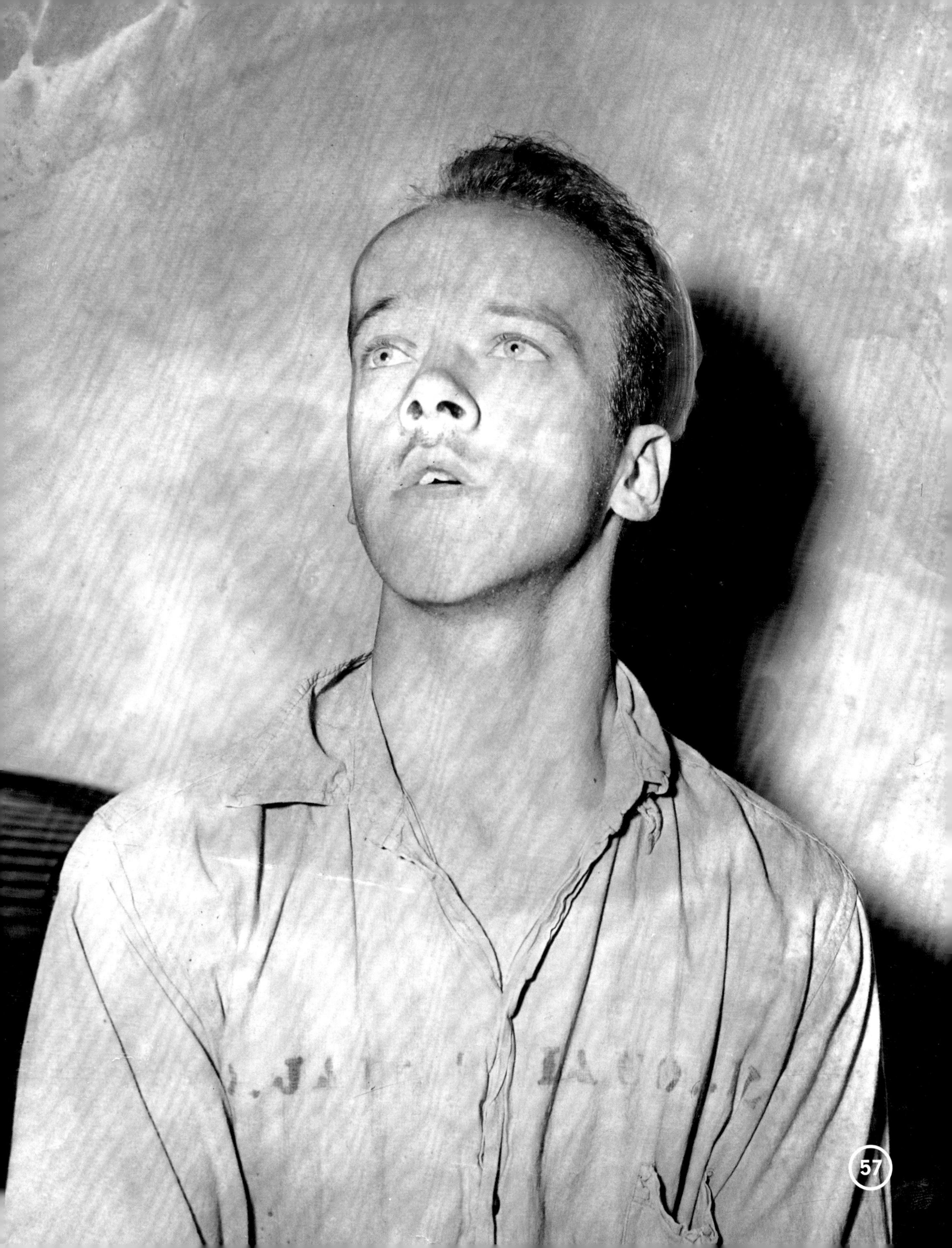

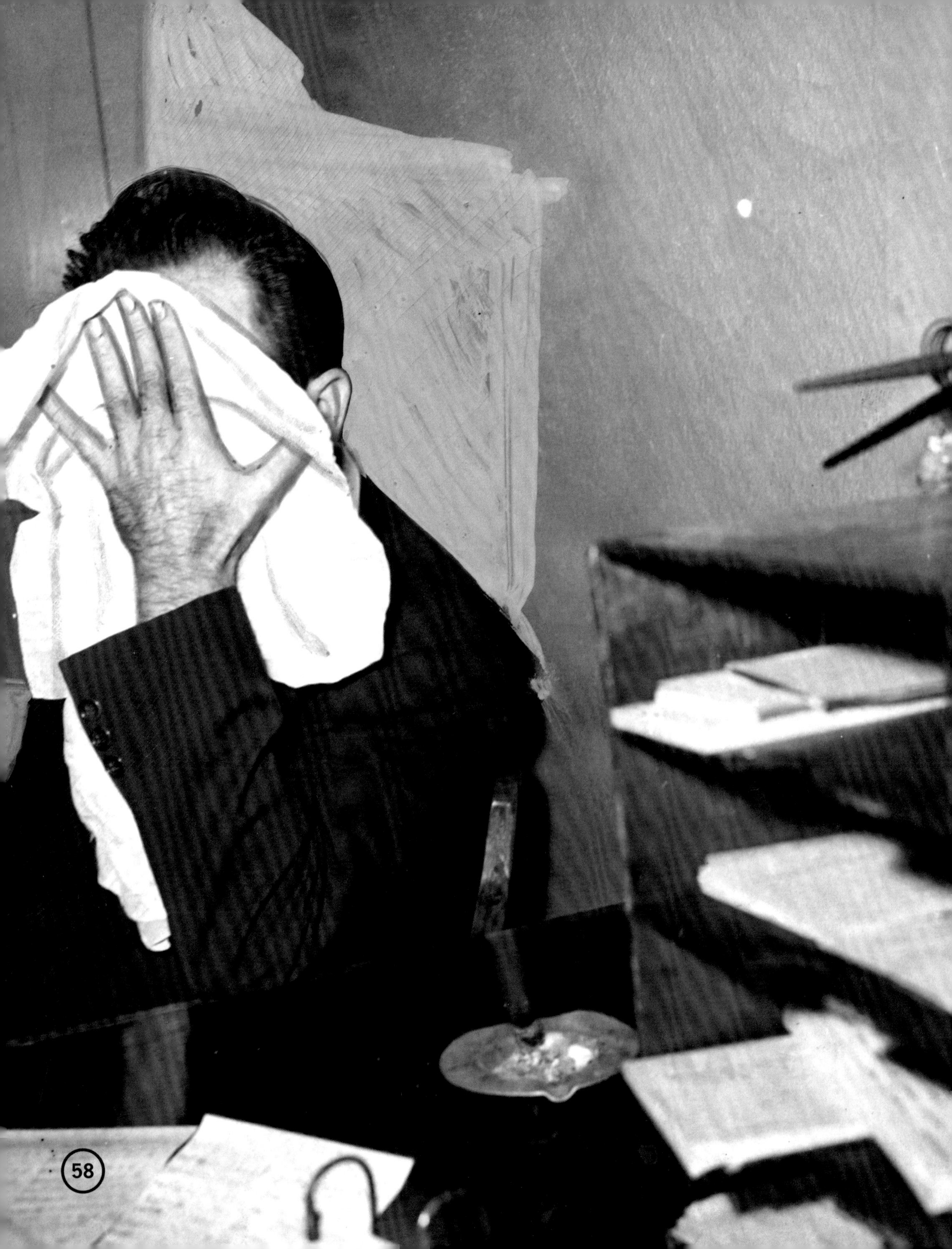

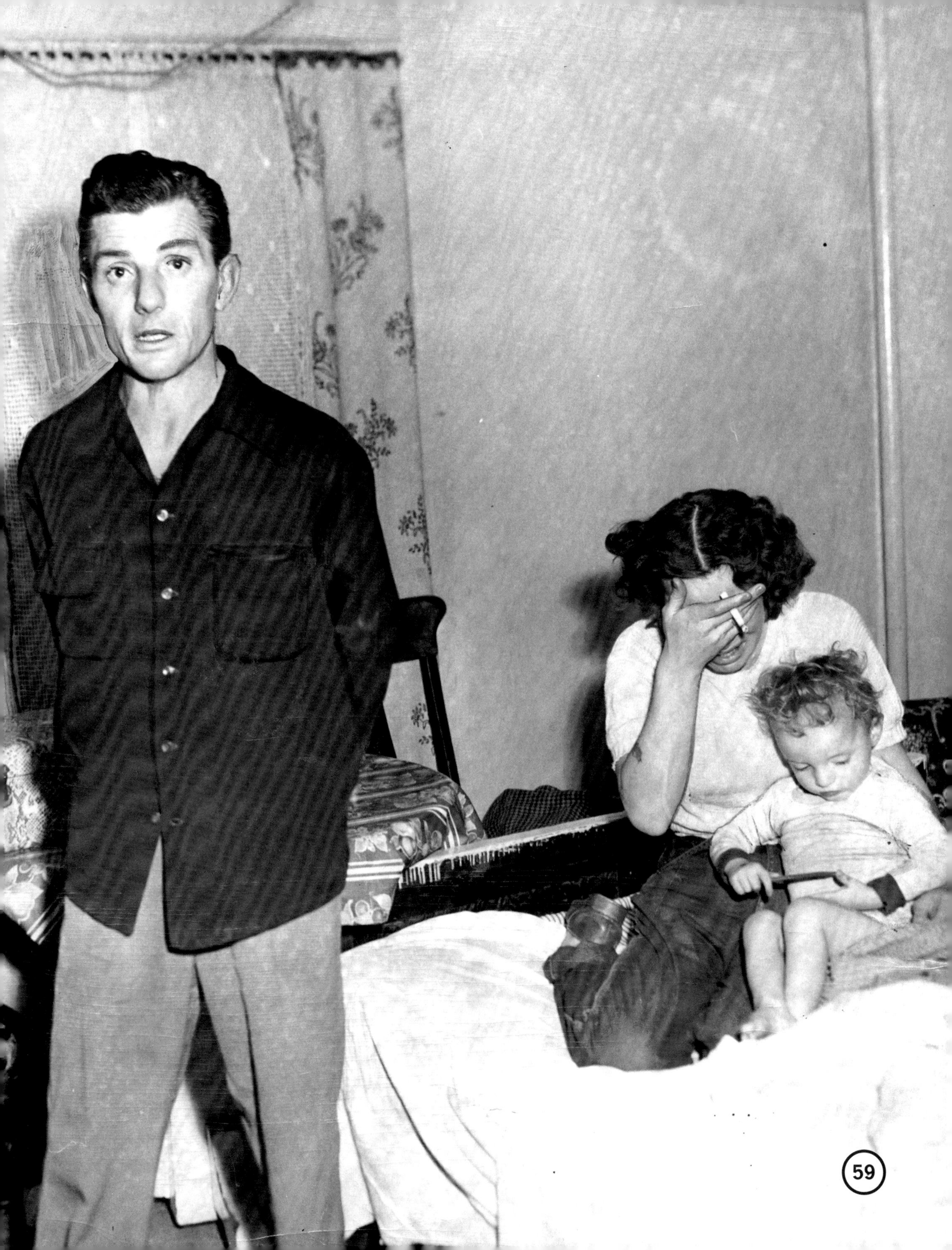

ON

TRIAL

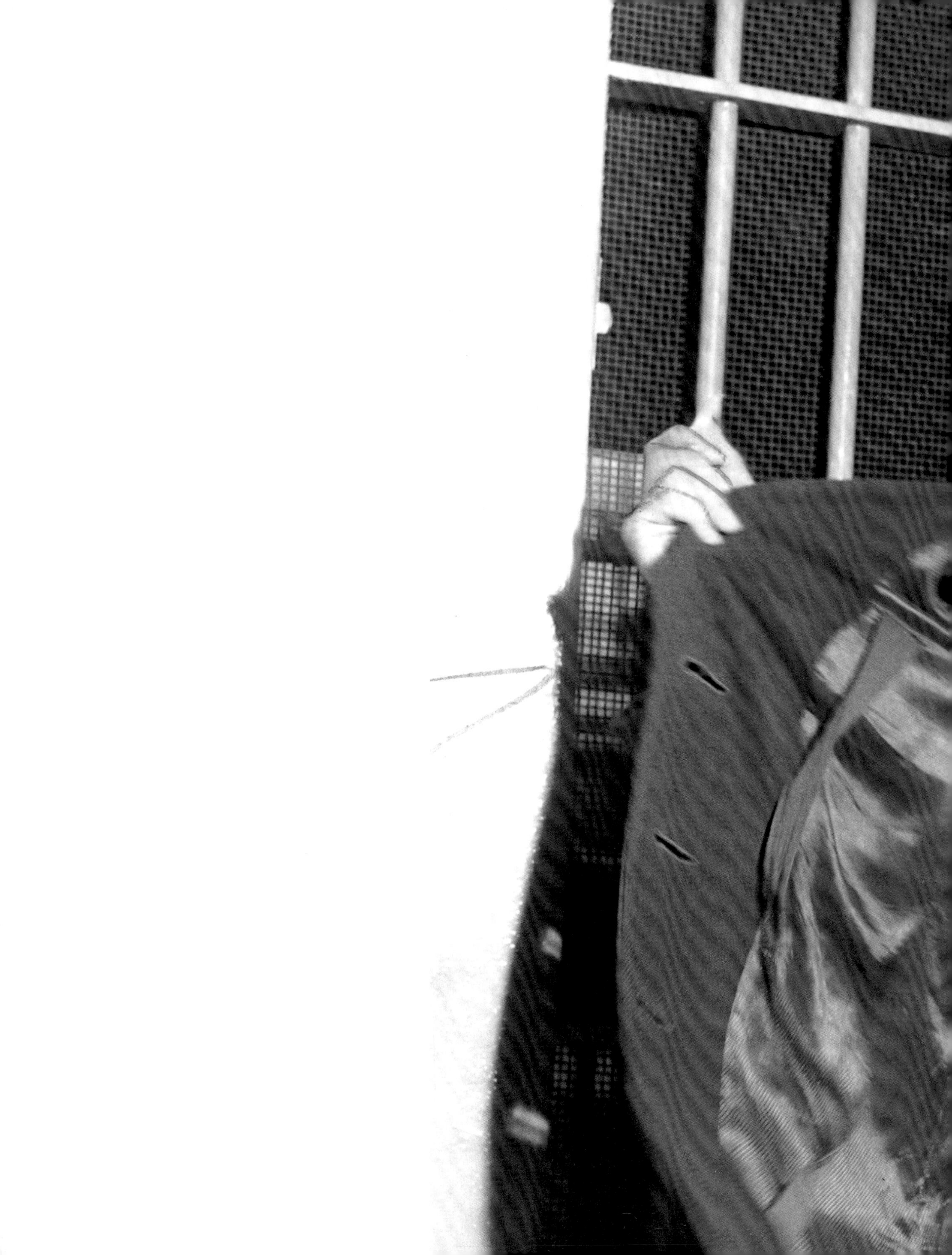

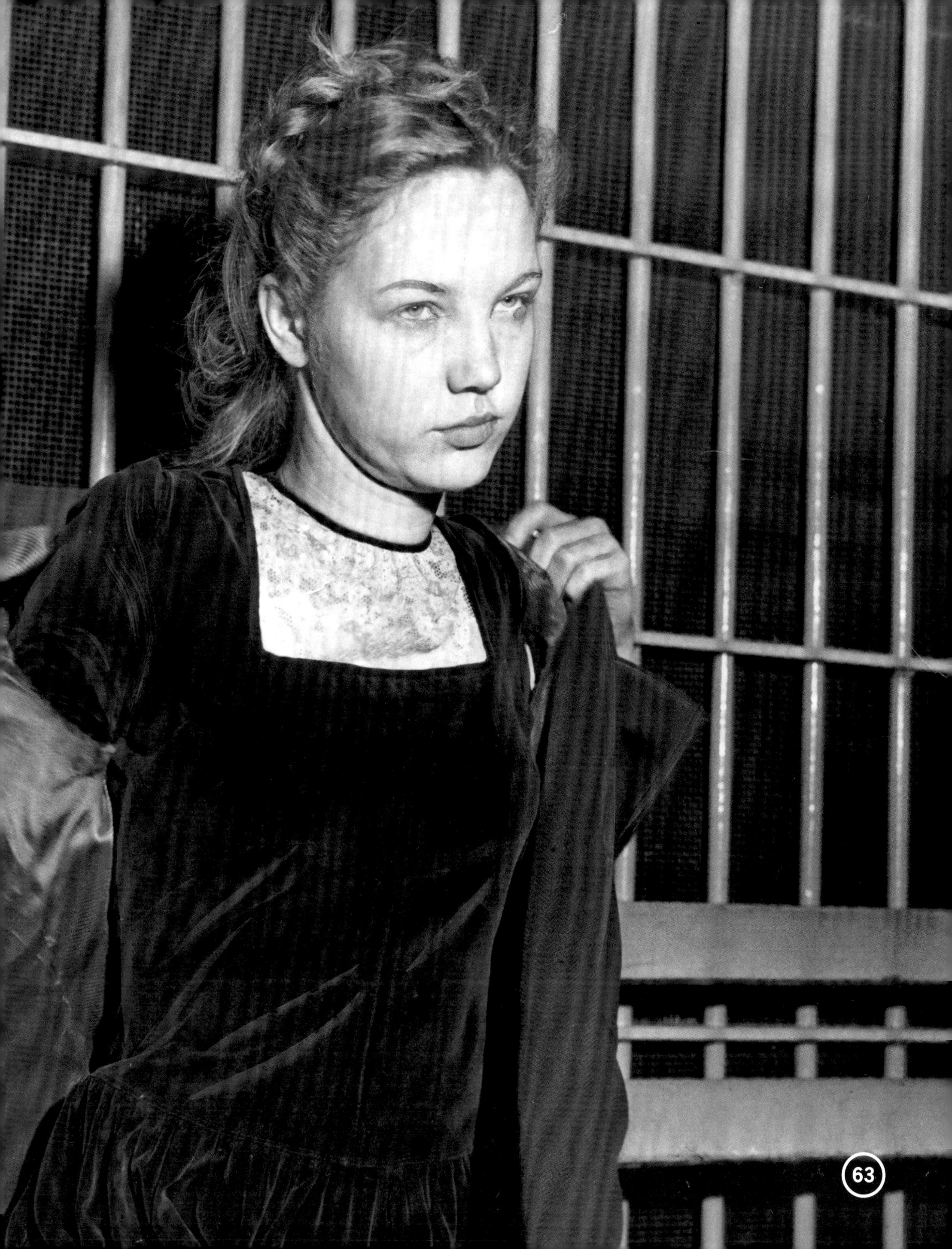

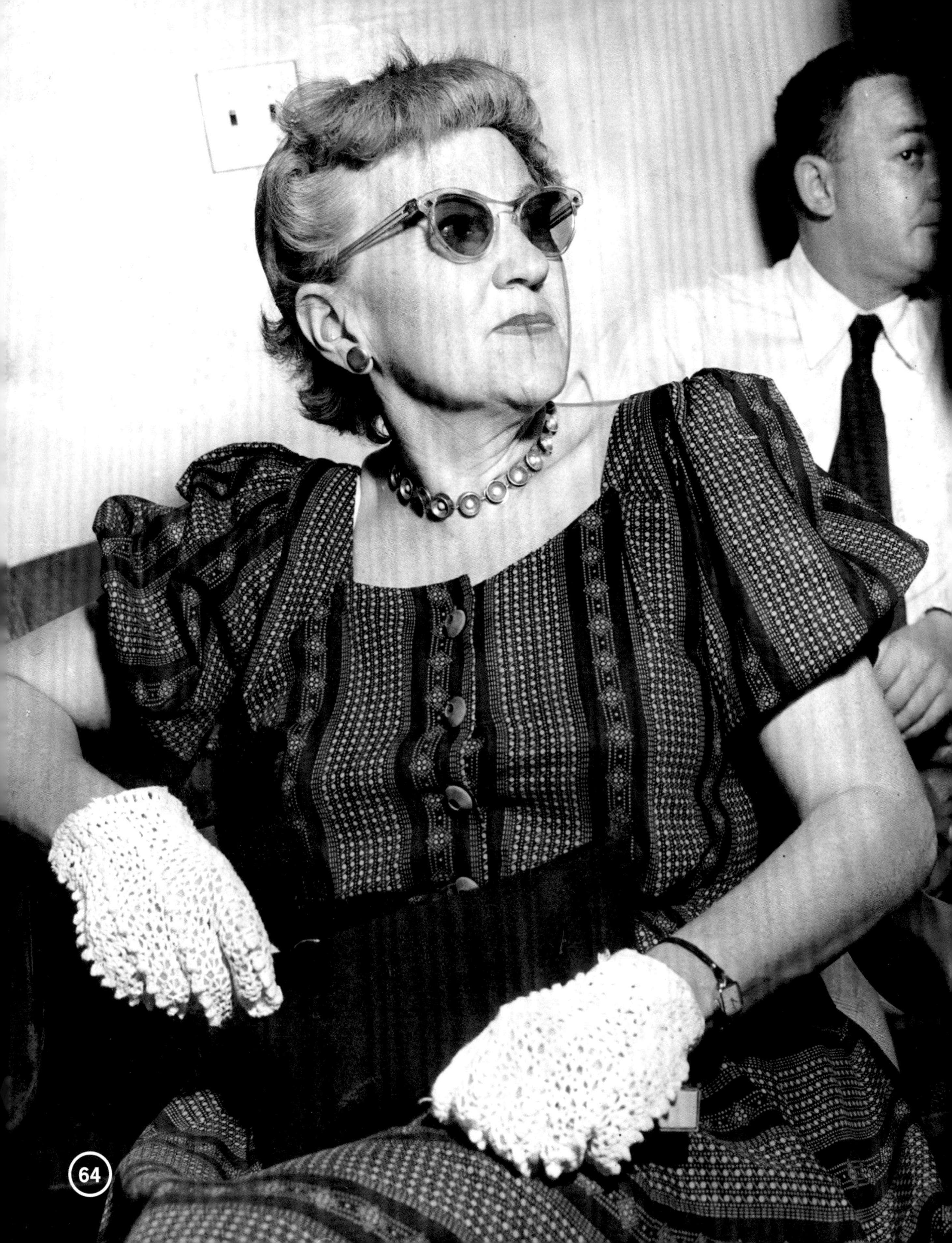

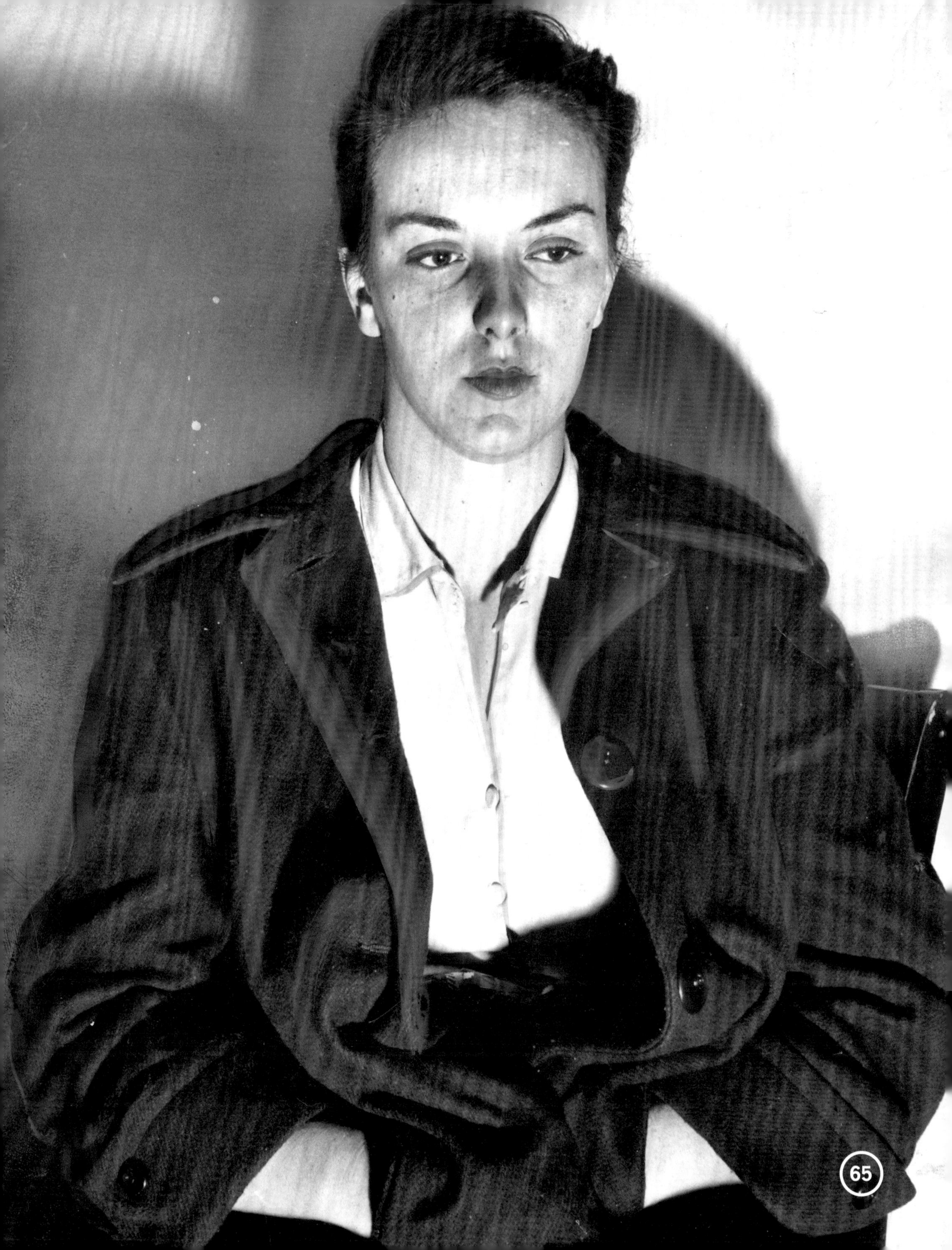

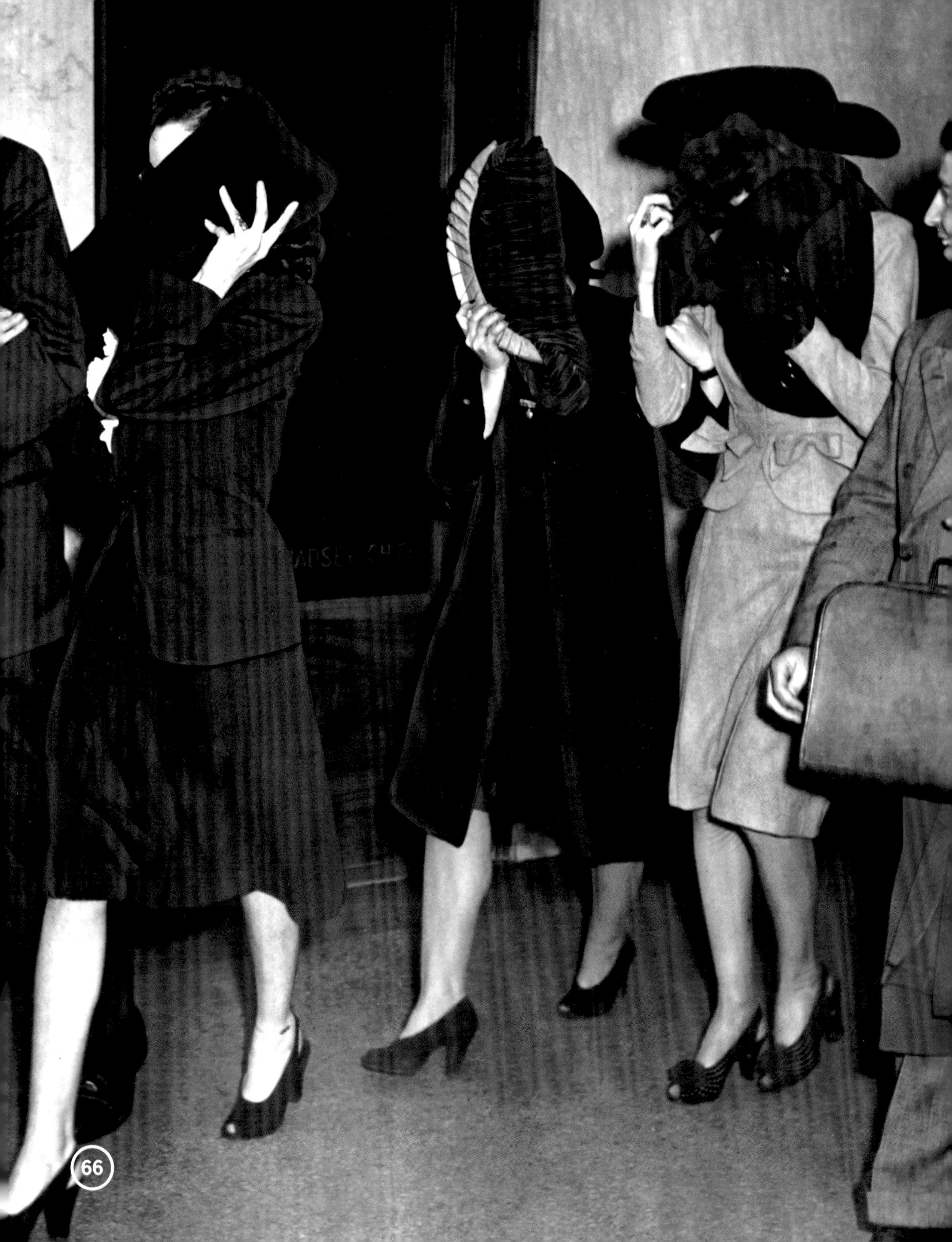

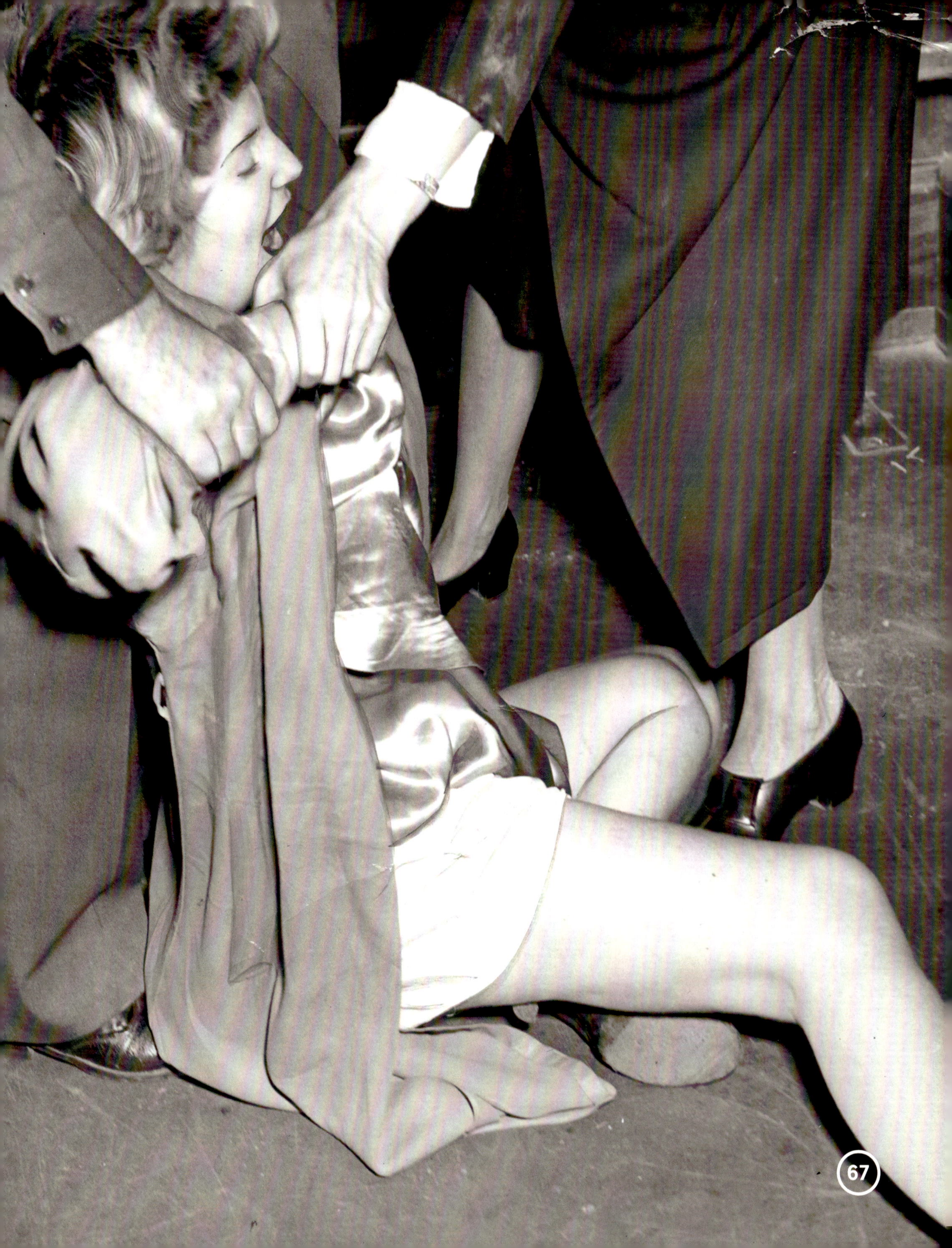

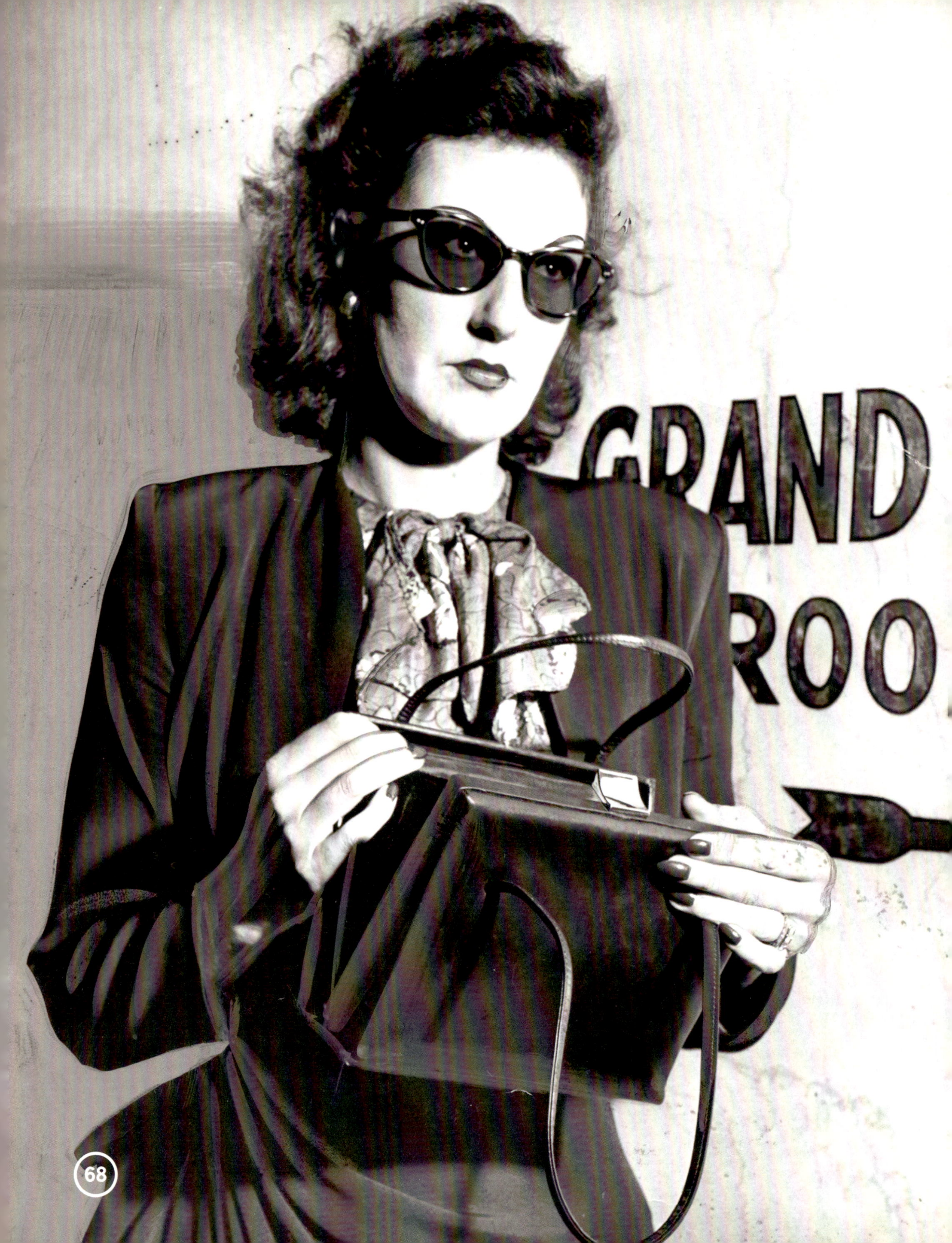
GRAND
ROO

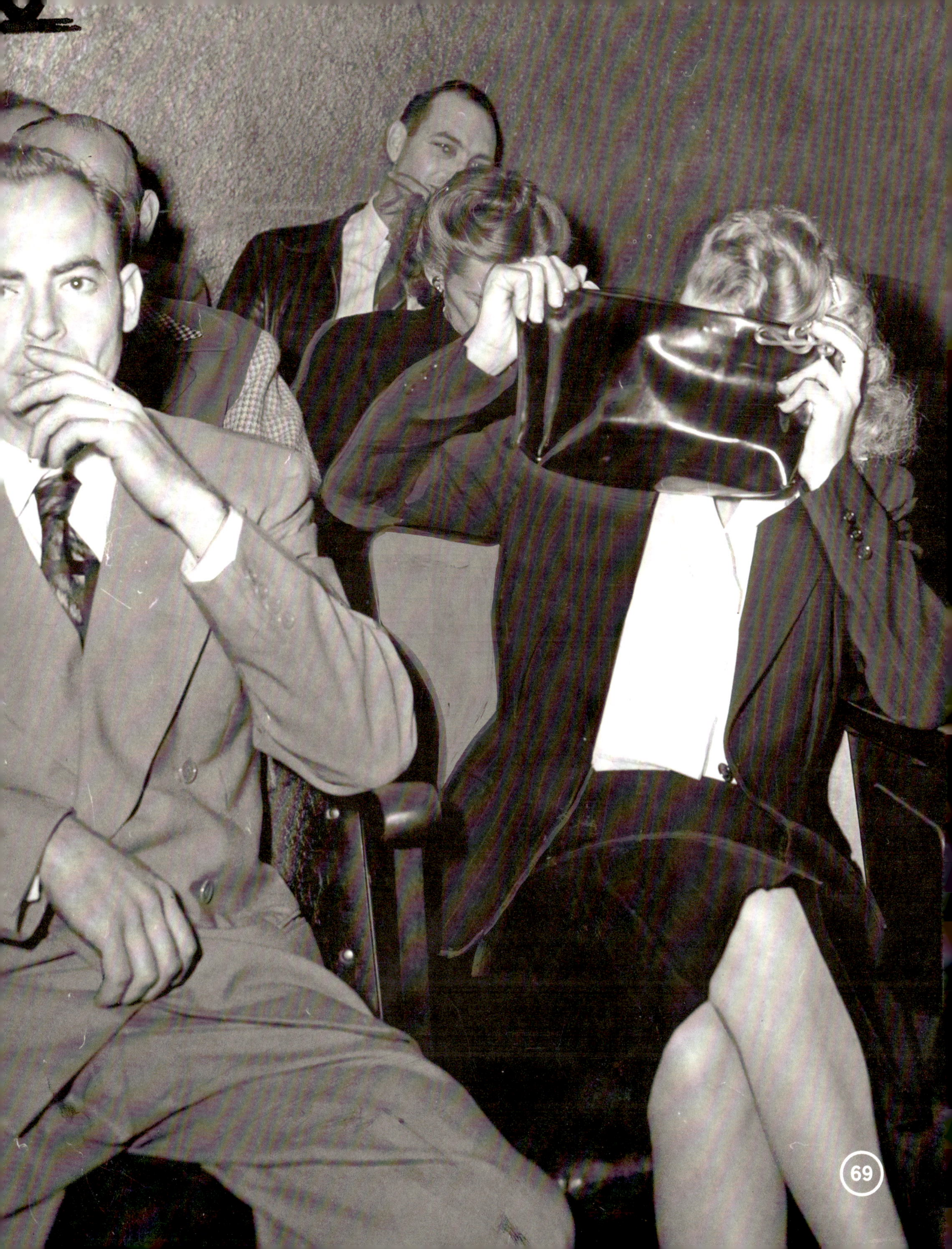

MURDERERS

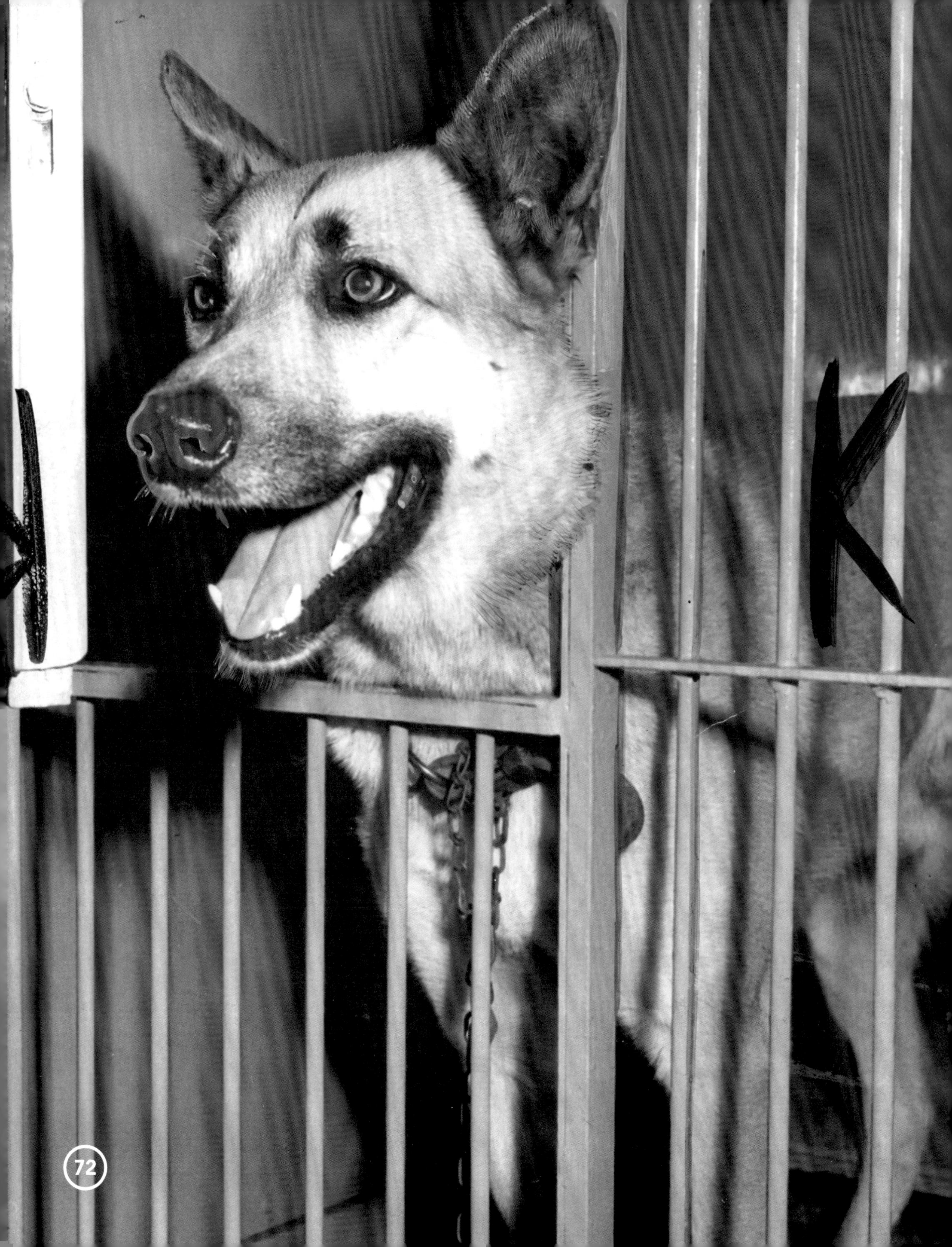

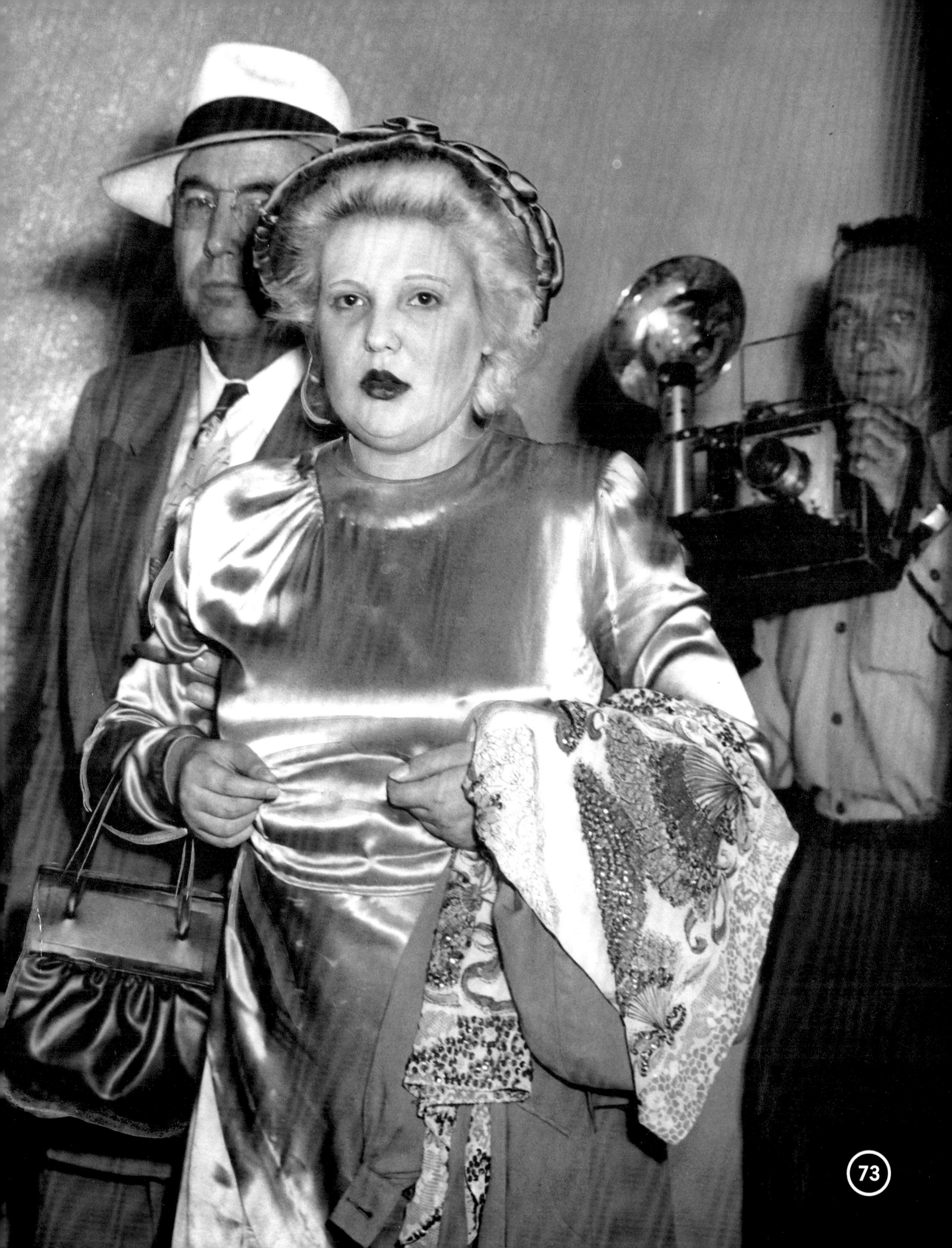

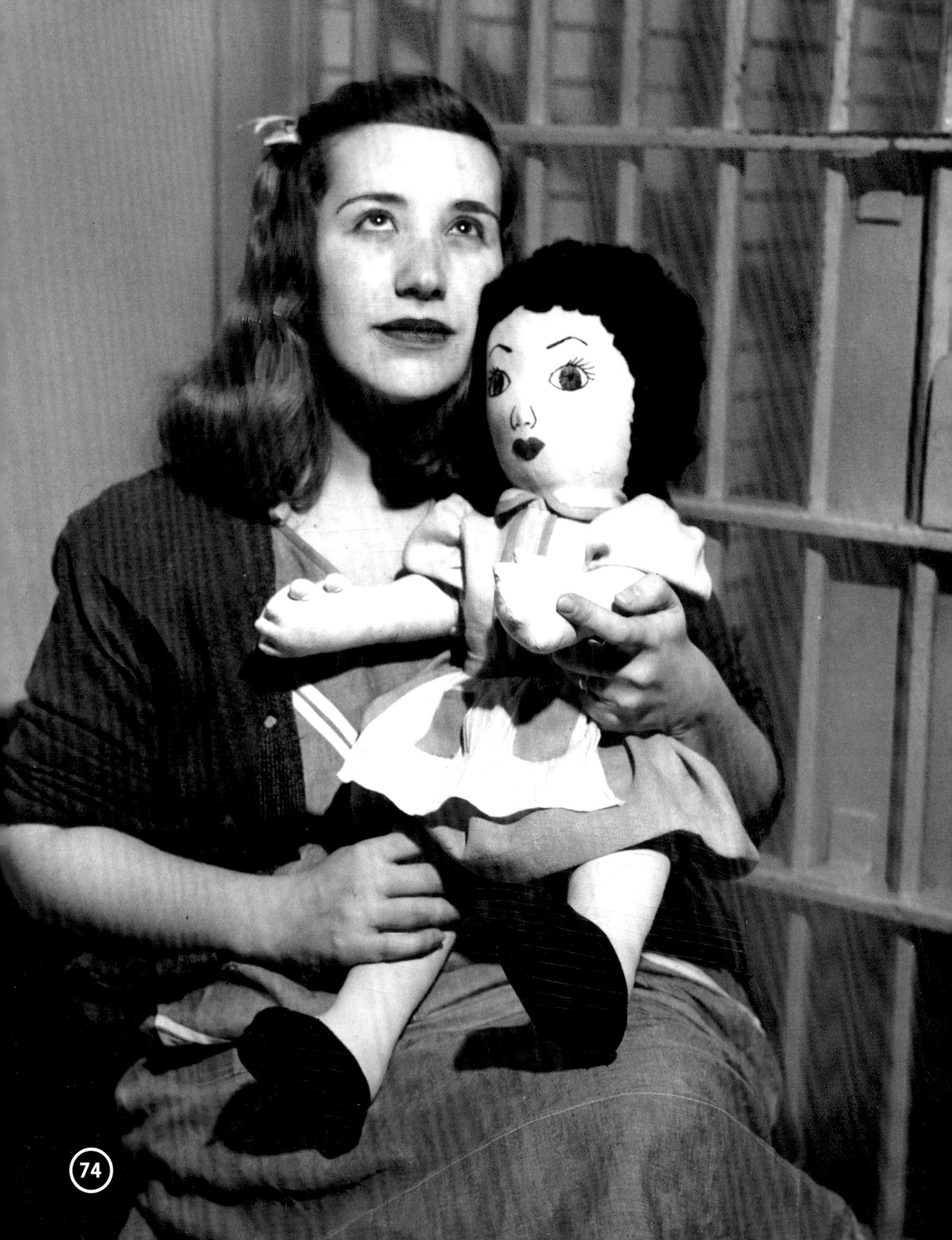

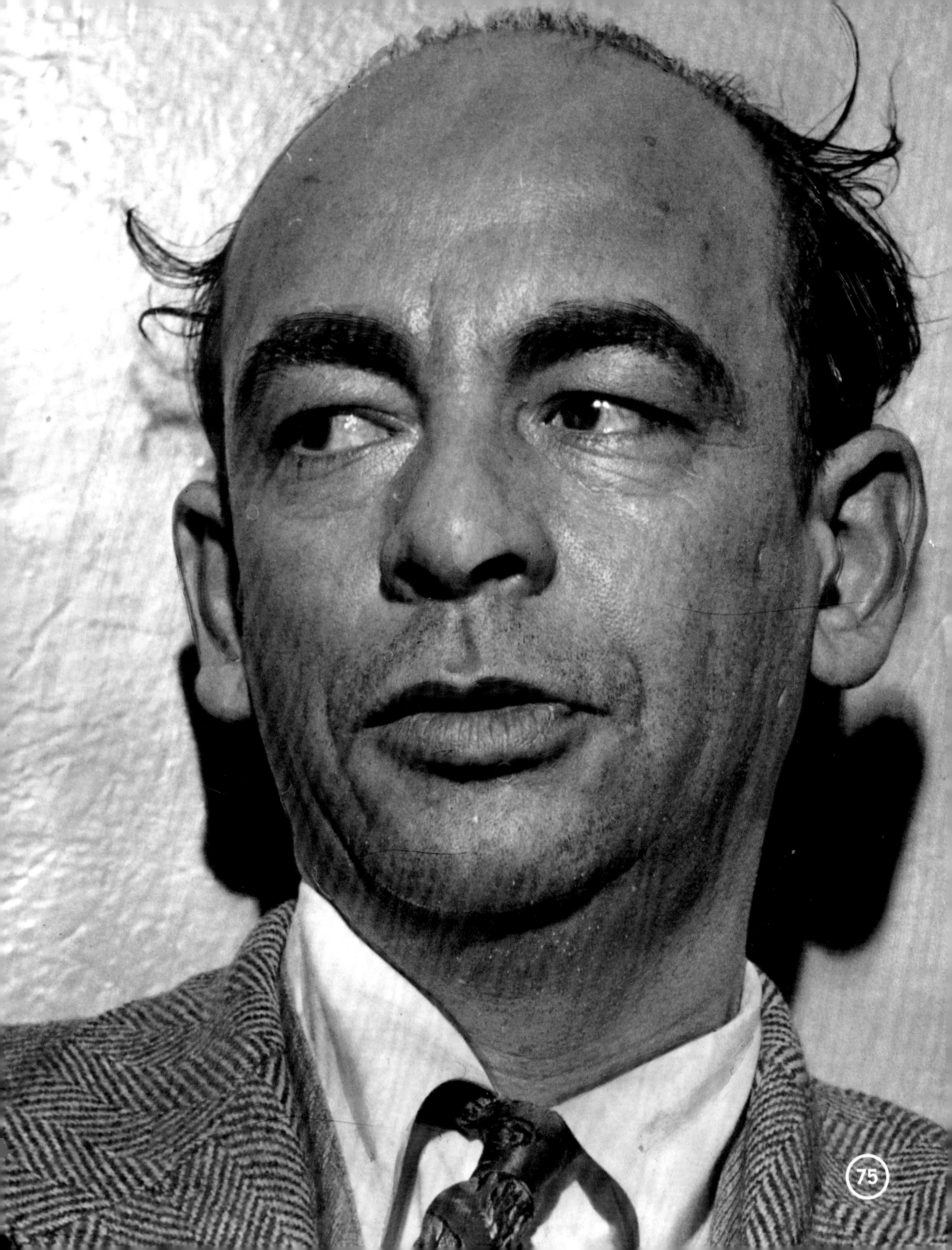

75

CITY

PORTRAITS

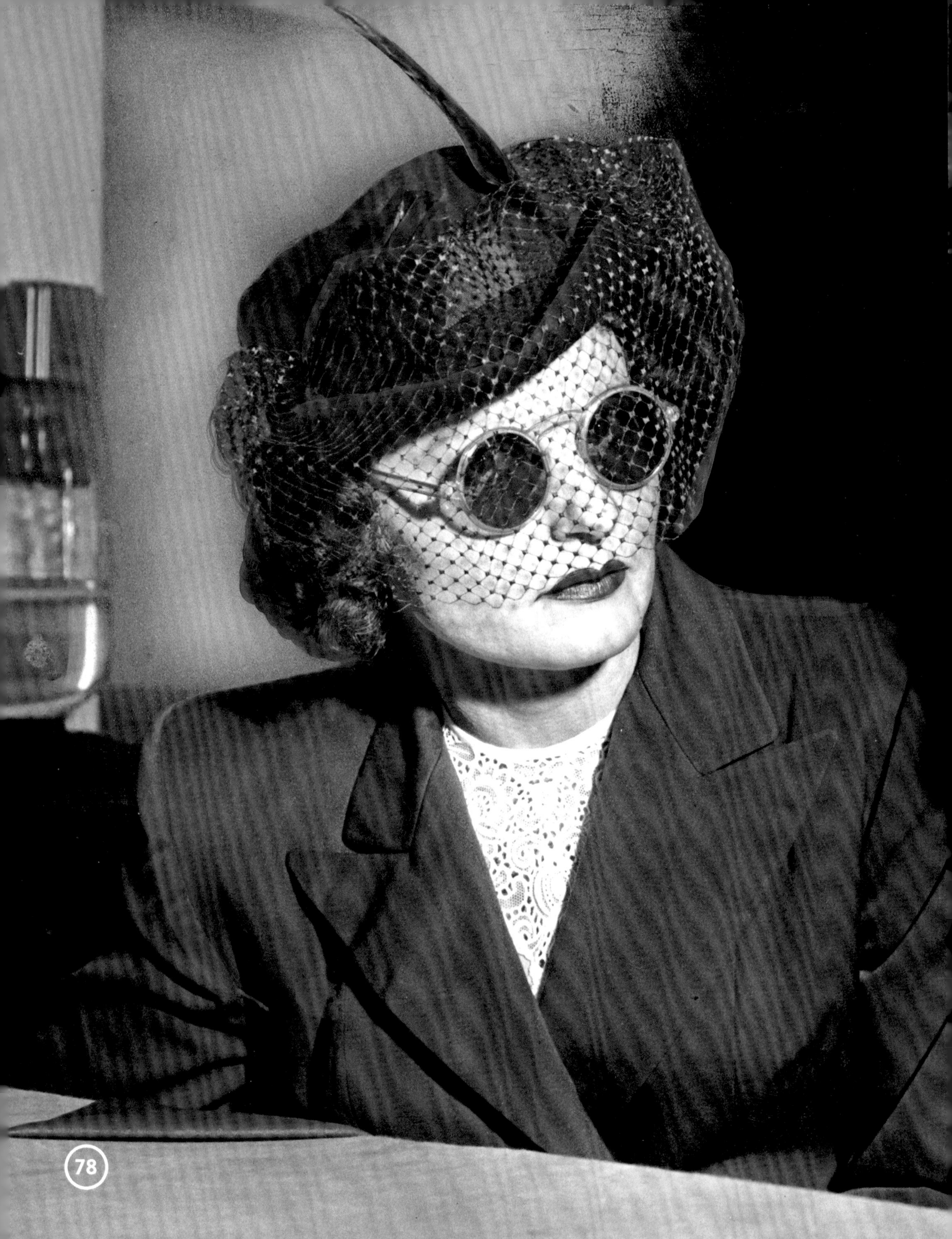

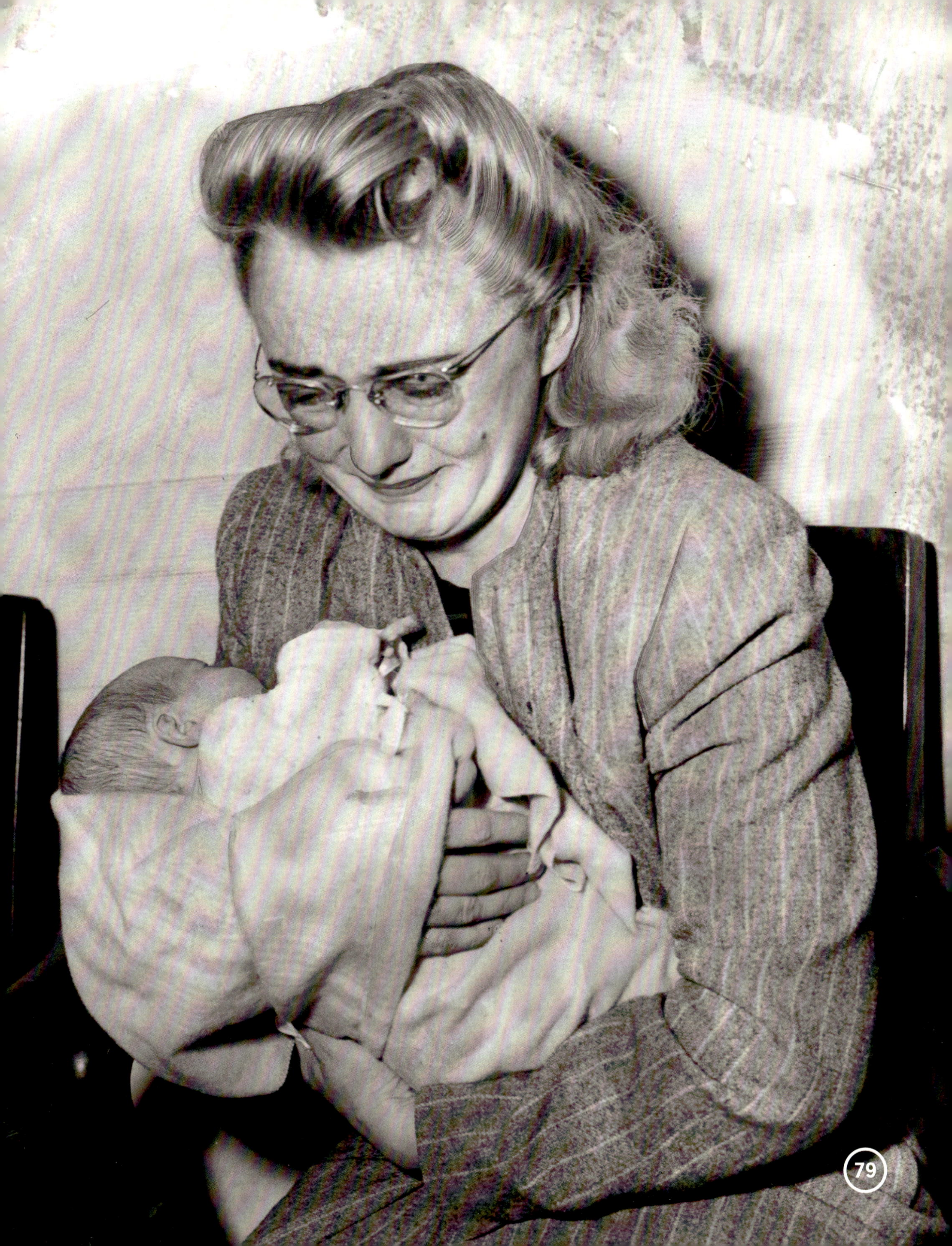

79

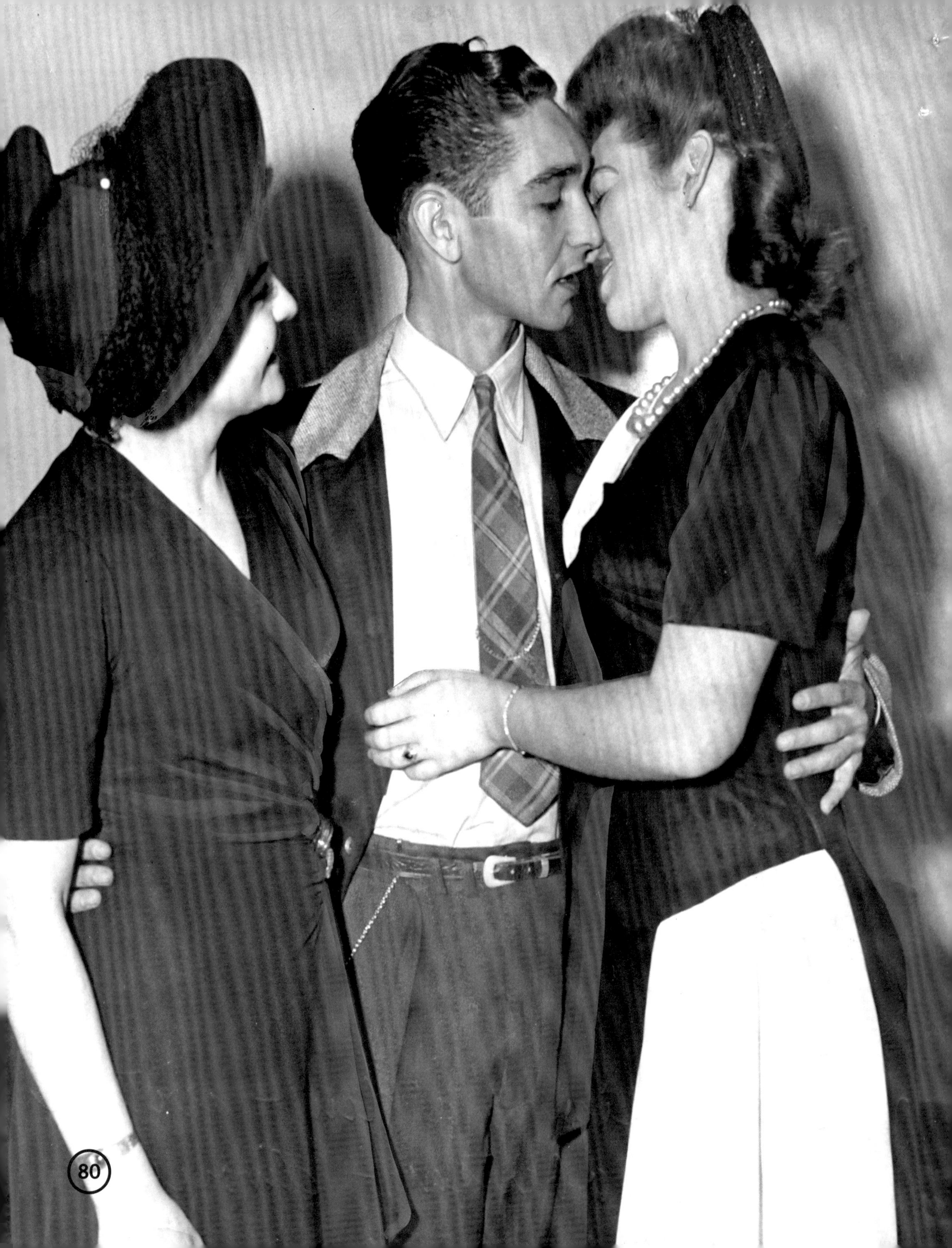

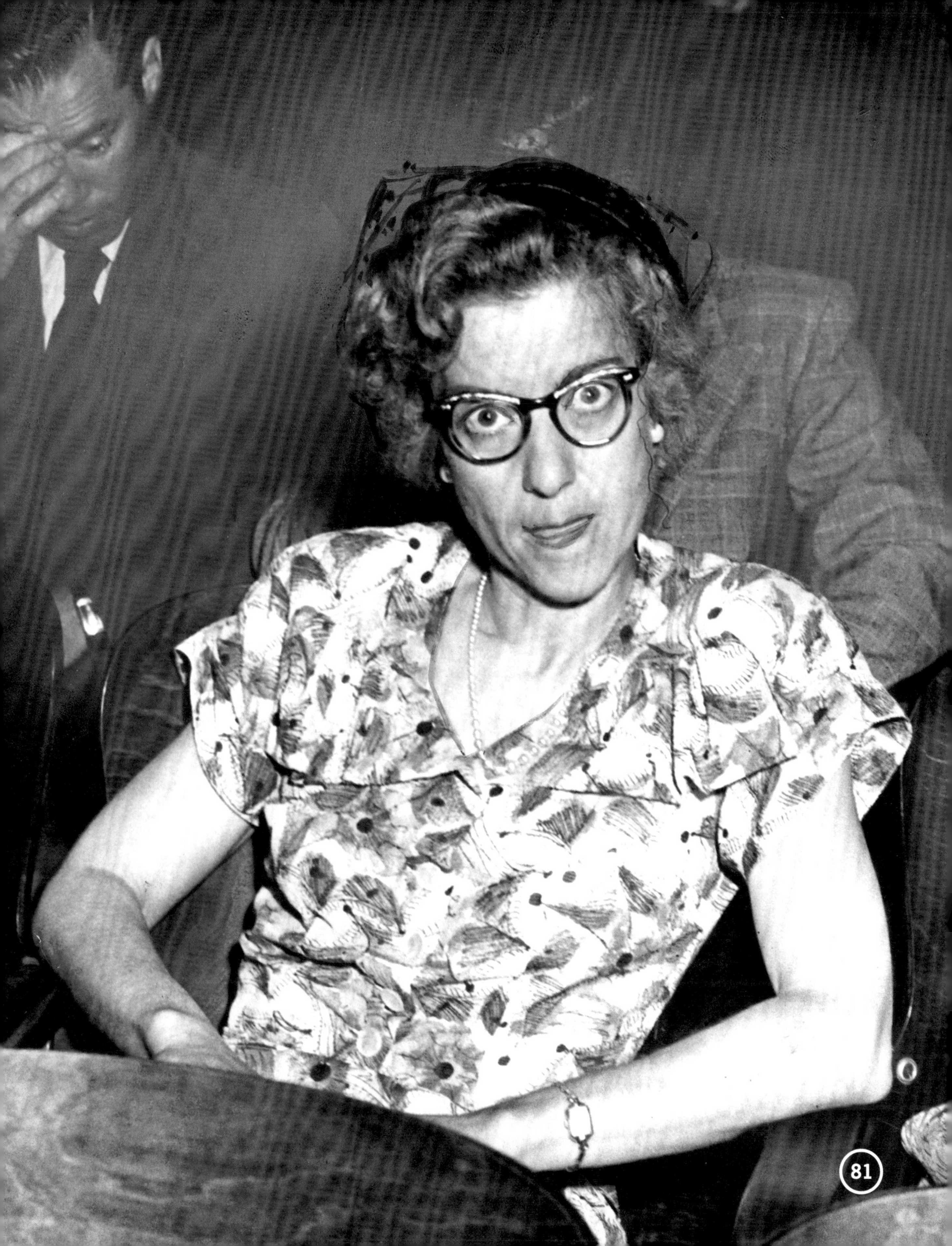
81

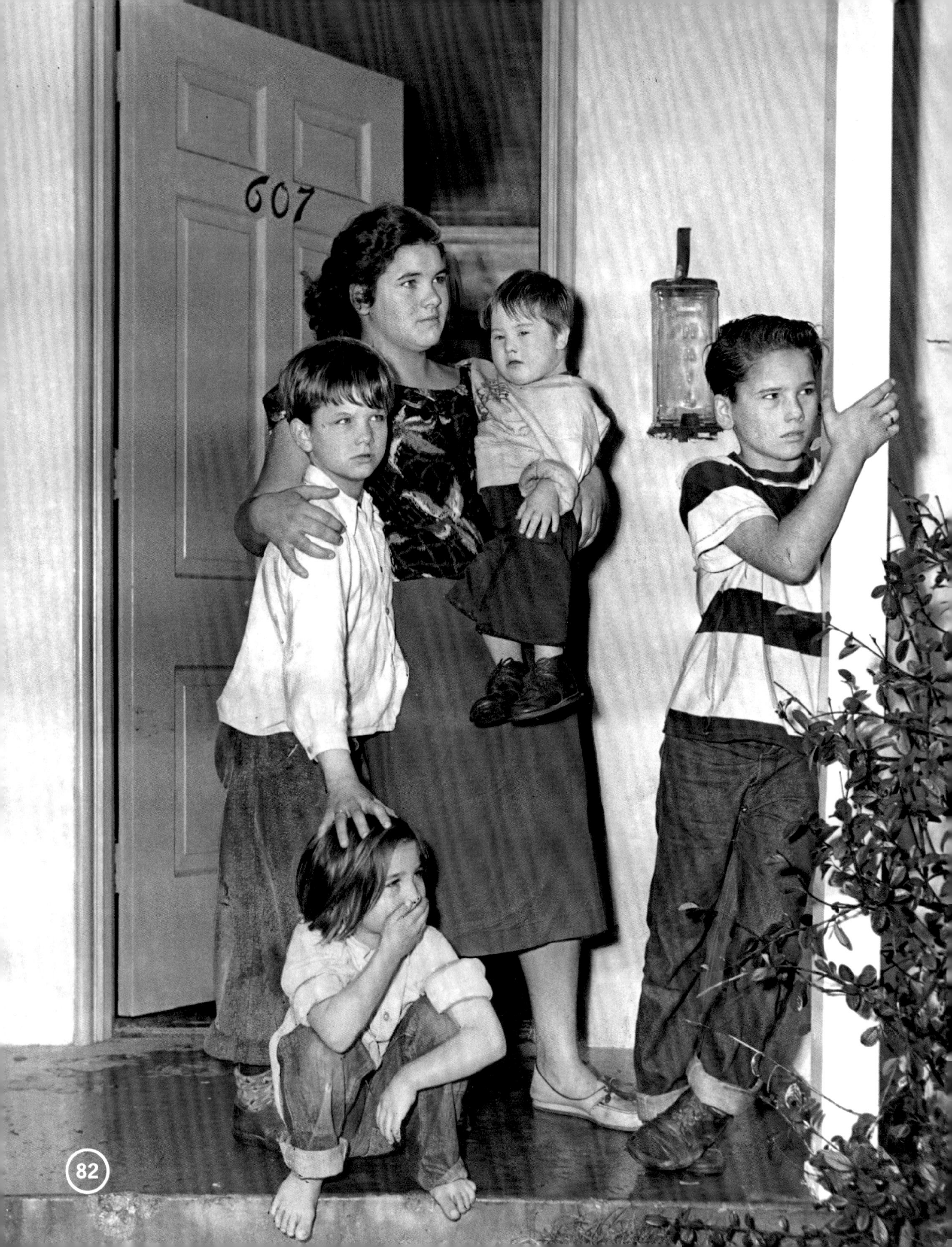
607

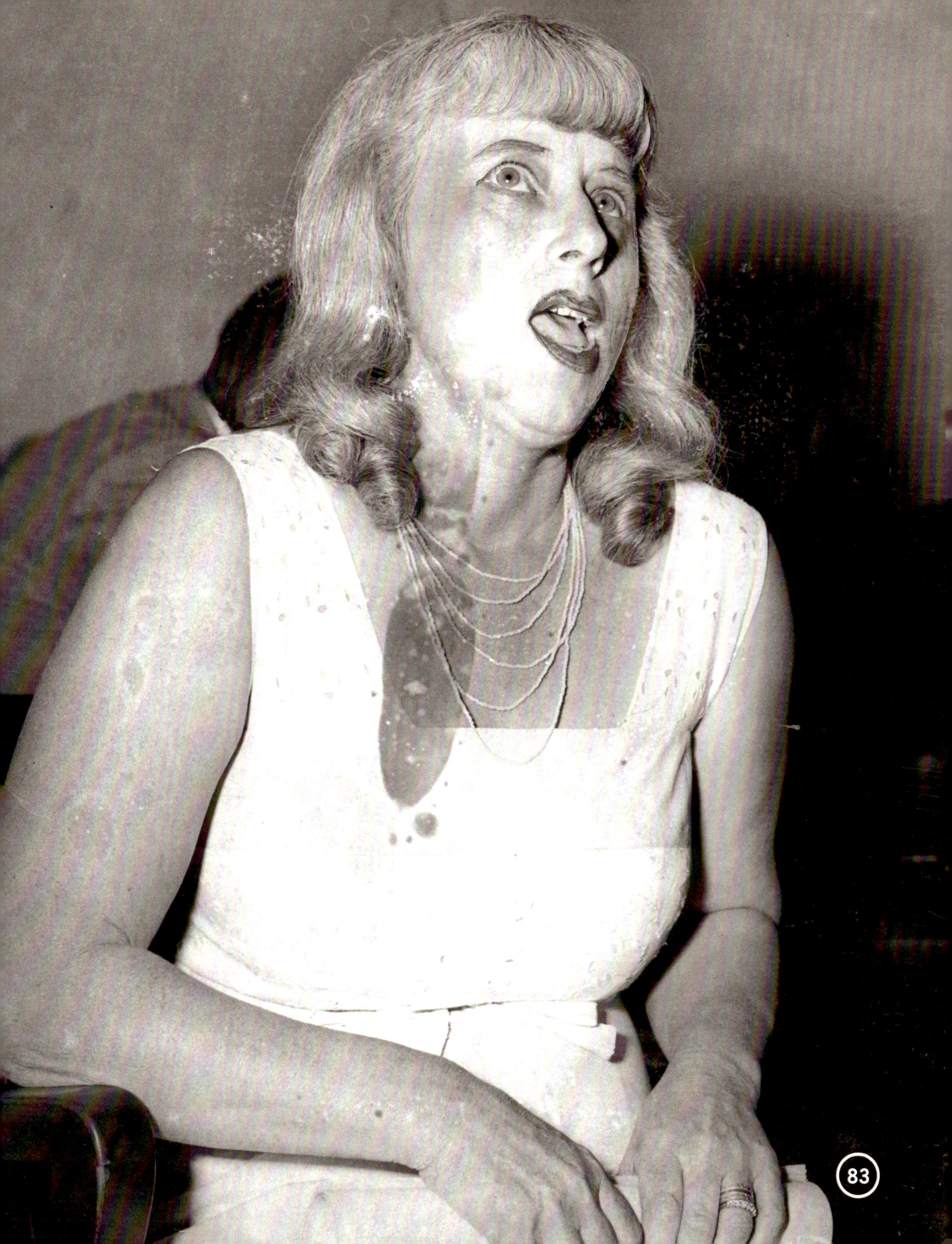

"HOUSE OF

(86) **MARY REICHEL**
MARCH 18, 1948 THURSDAY

"House of Horror" victim gets cleaned up

(87) **MARIE CLAVEY**
DATE UNKNOWN

Faces new investigation as "Horror House" home allegedly open

(88) JULY 16, 1948 FRIDAY

PAULINE MURPHY and mother, **MRS. MABEL MURPHY,** neighbors in "Horror House" trial

(89) MARCH 18, 1948 THURSDAY

JOHN J. WAYNE, 11, first "slave" discovered in case, was all bones and little flesh. His discovery led police to "House of Horror" shack-prison

HORROR"

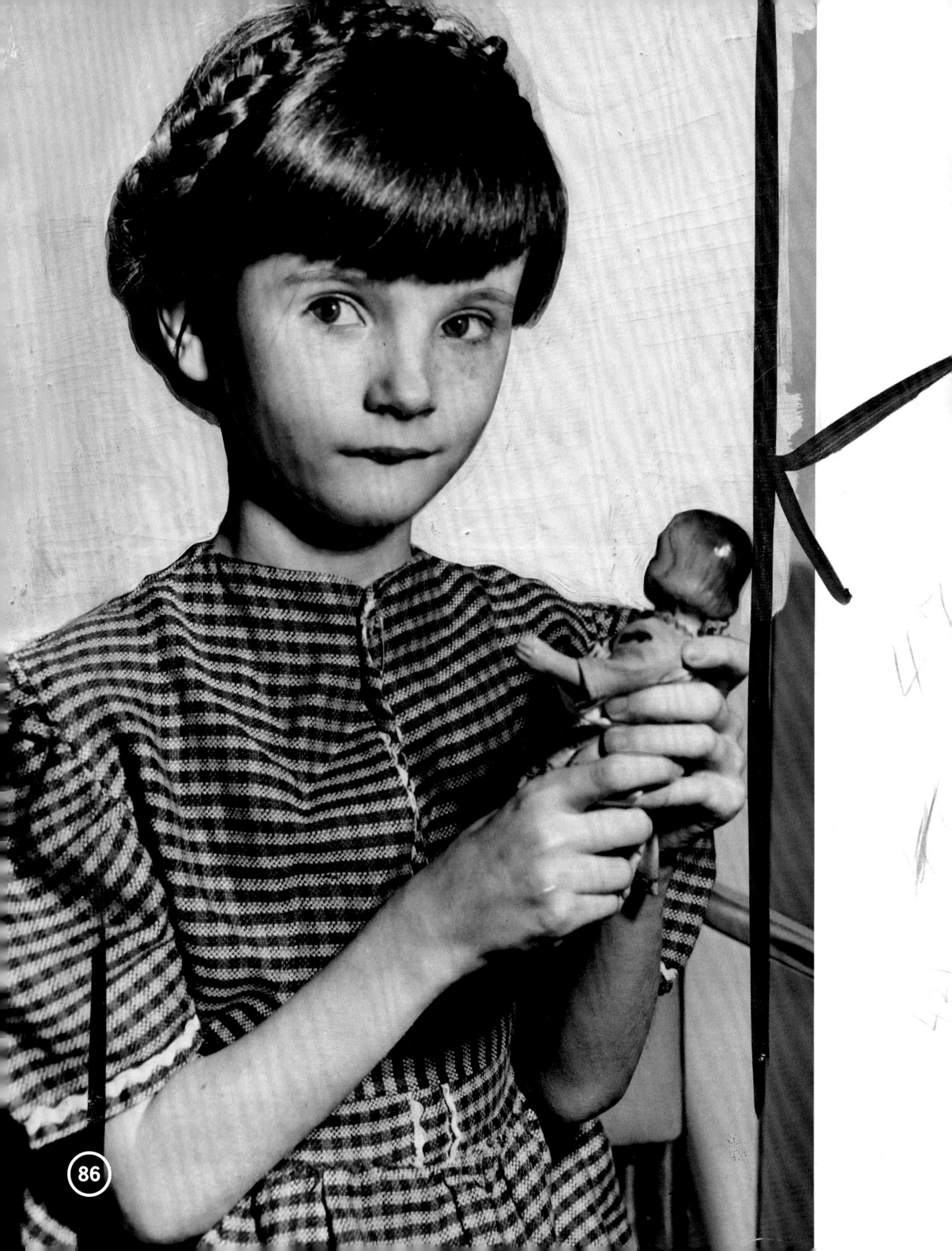

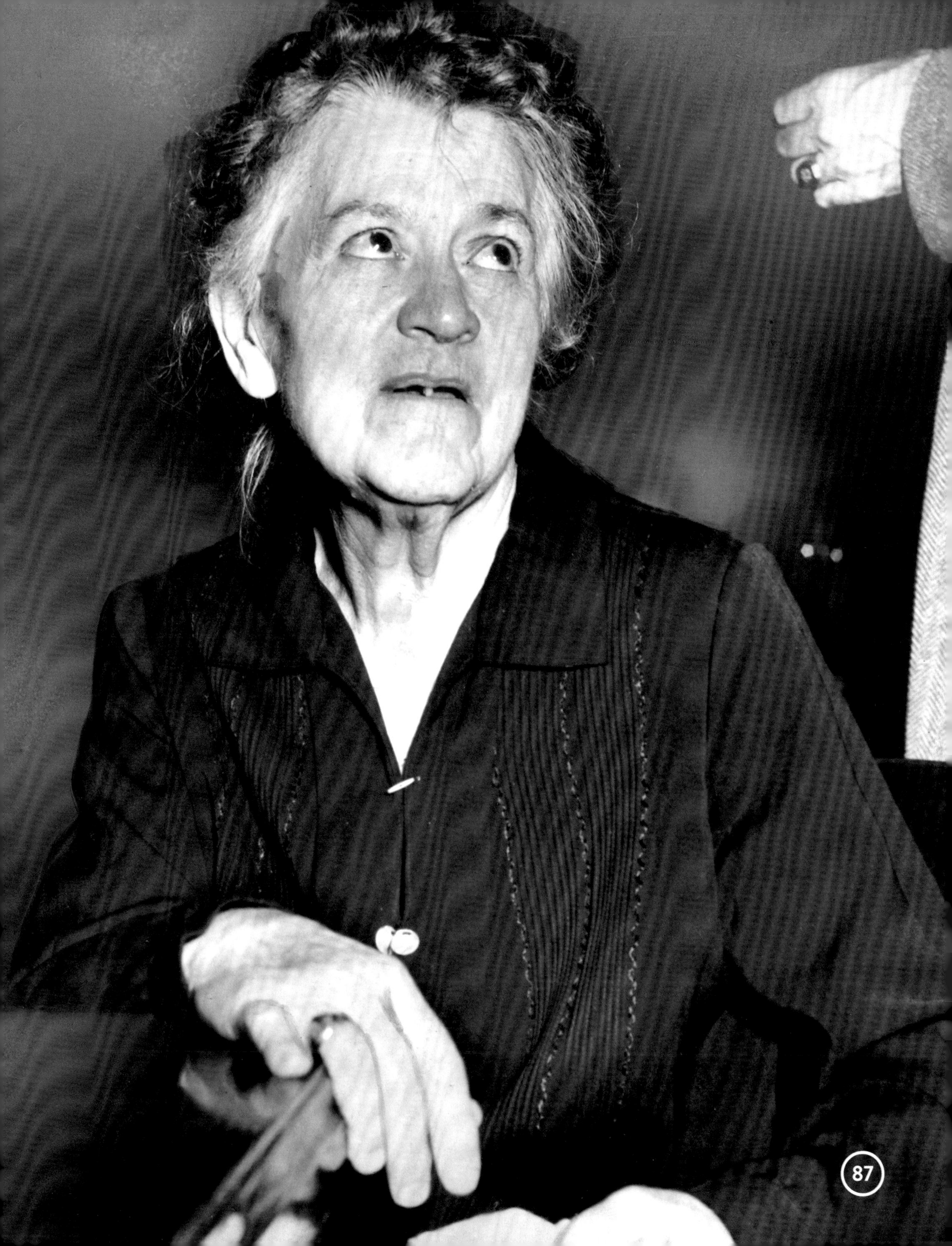

87

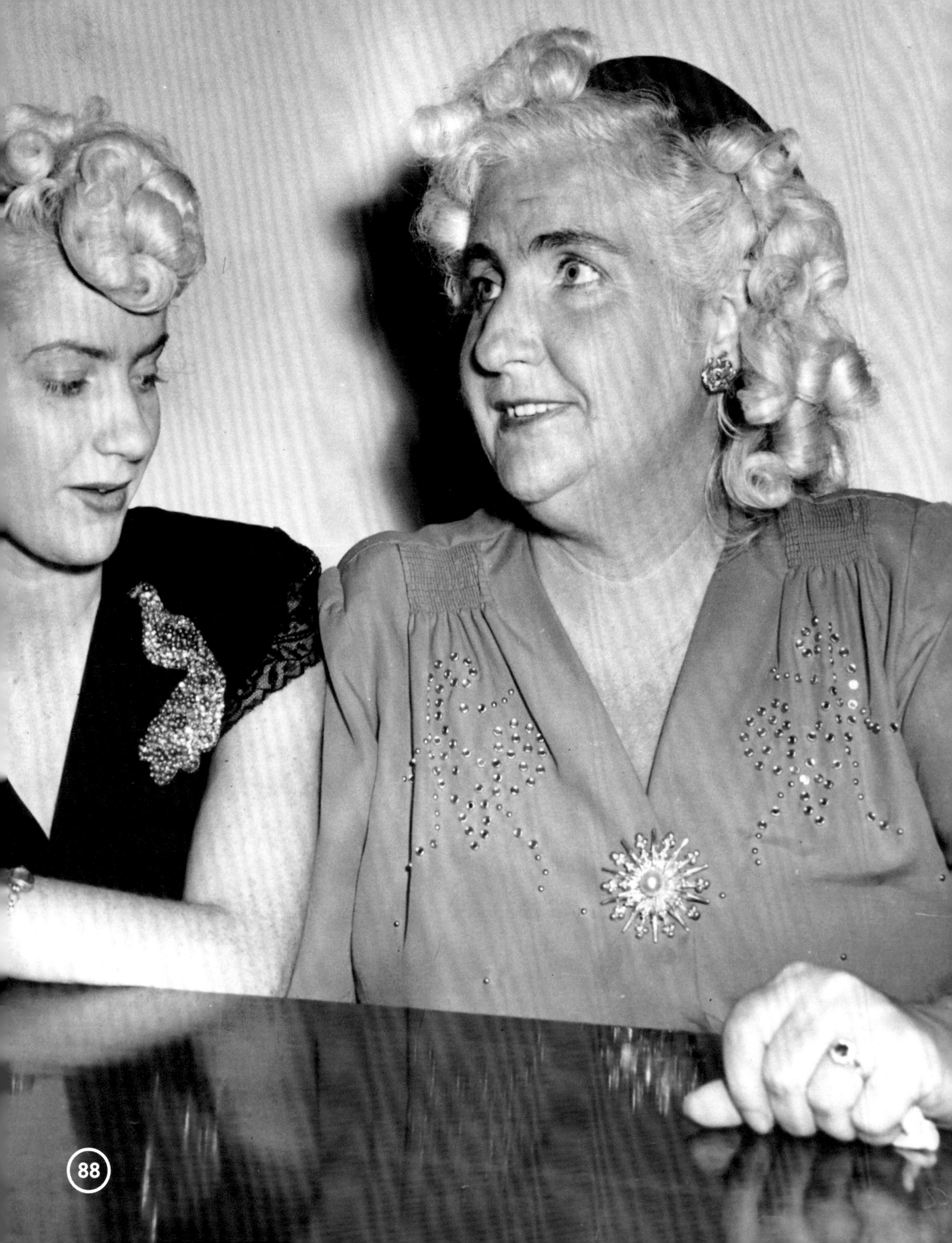

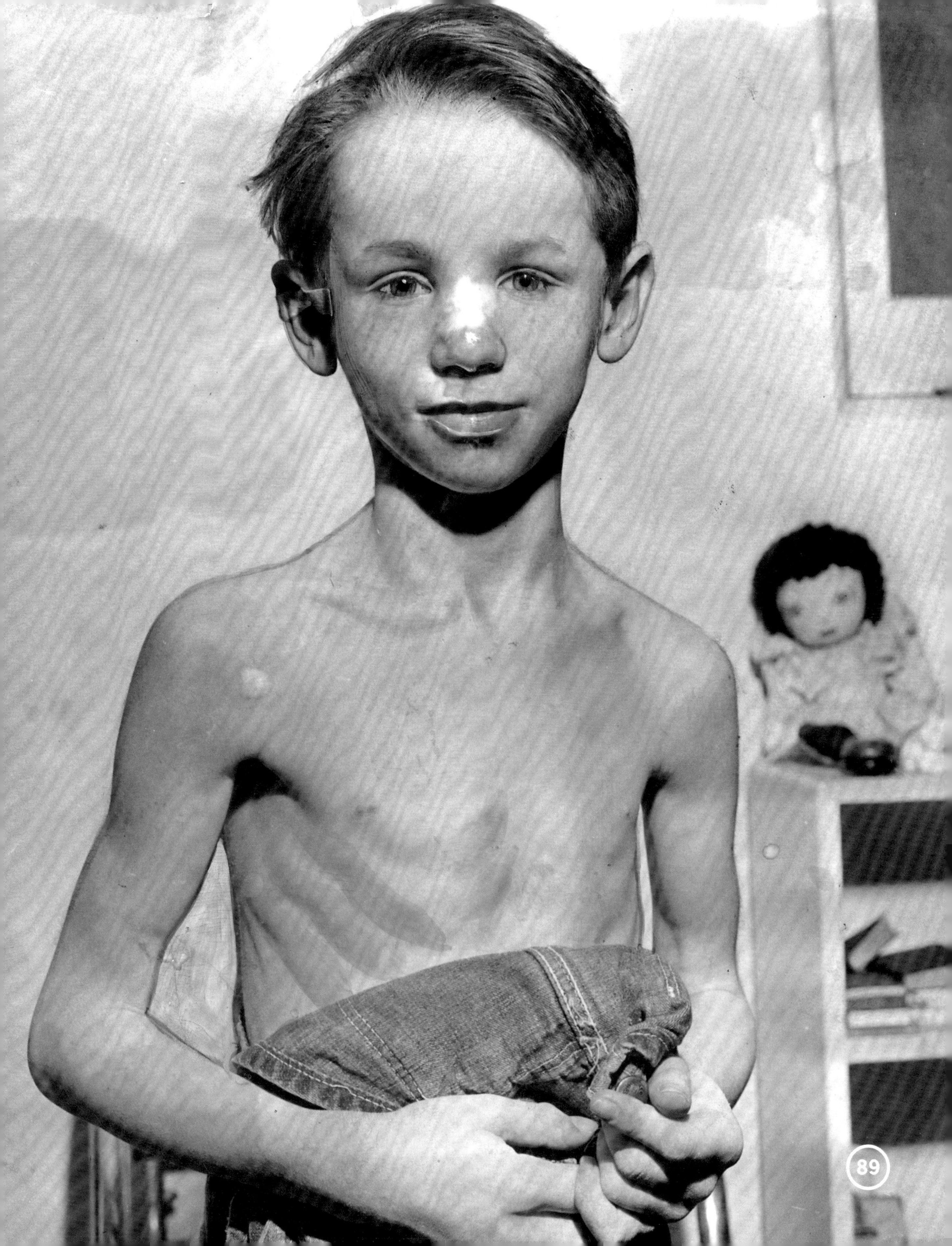

WHITE-OUTS

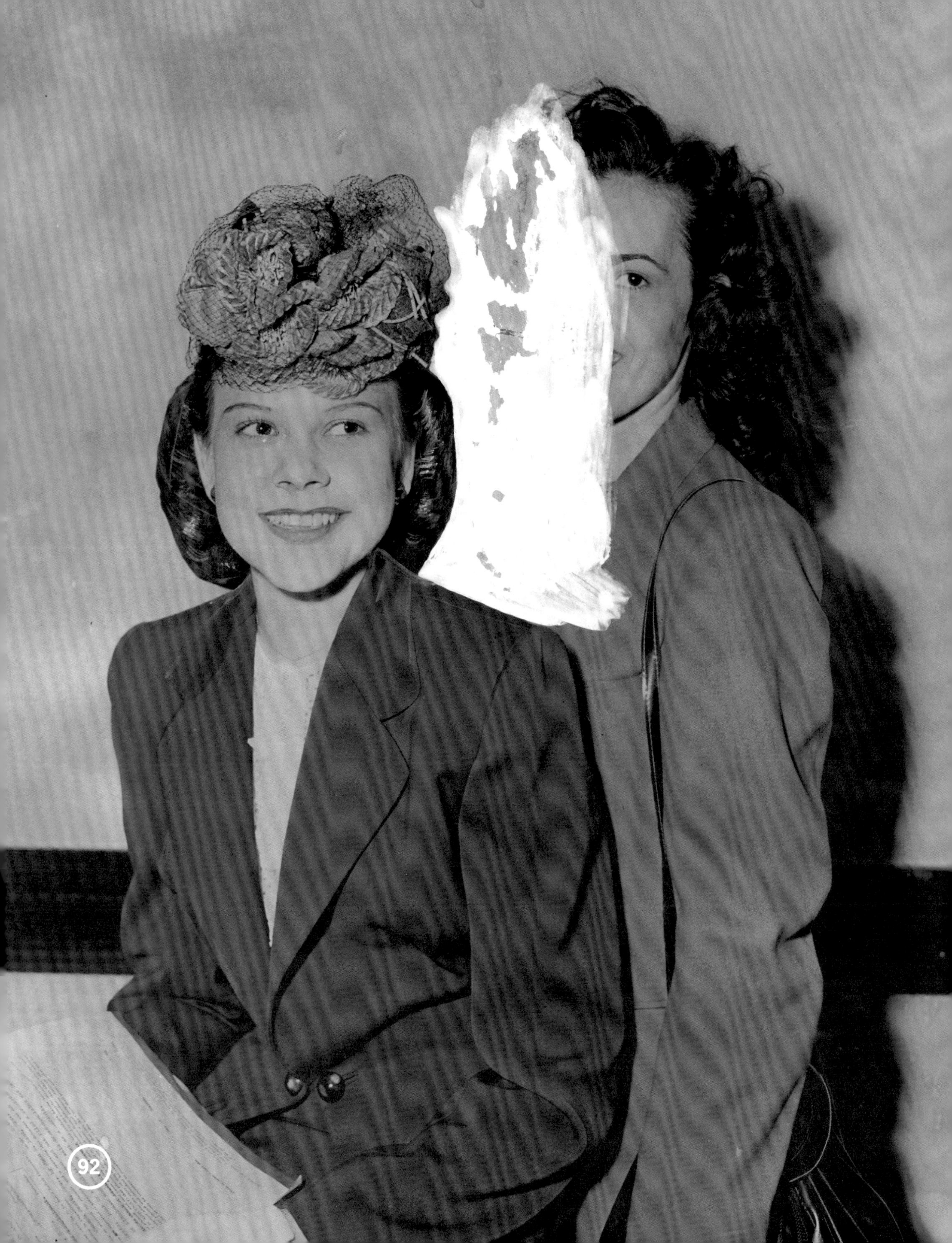

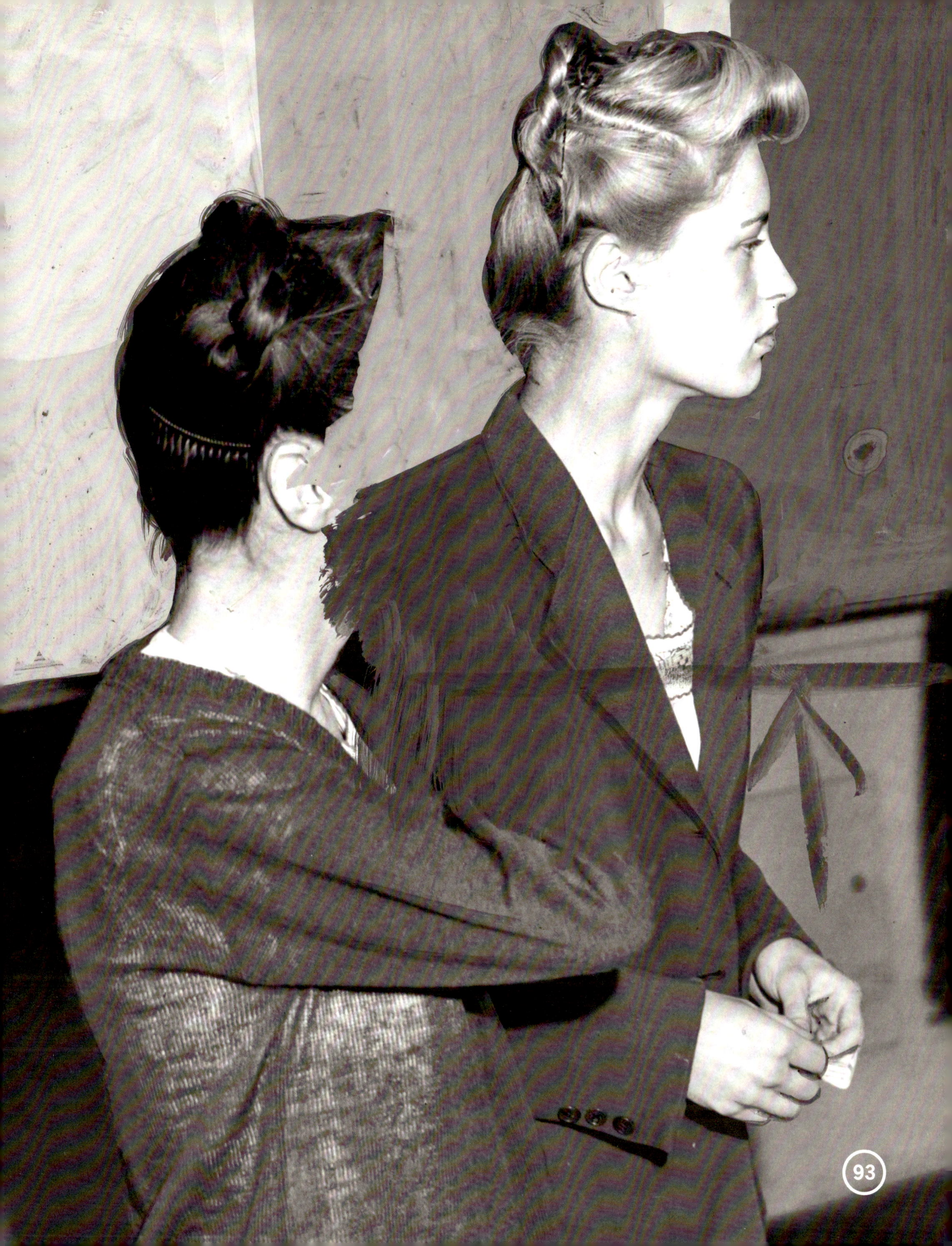

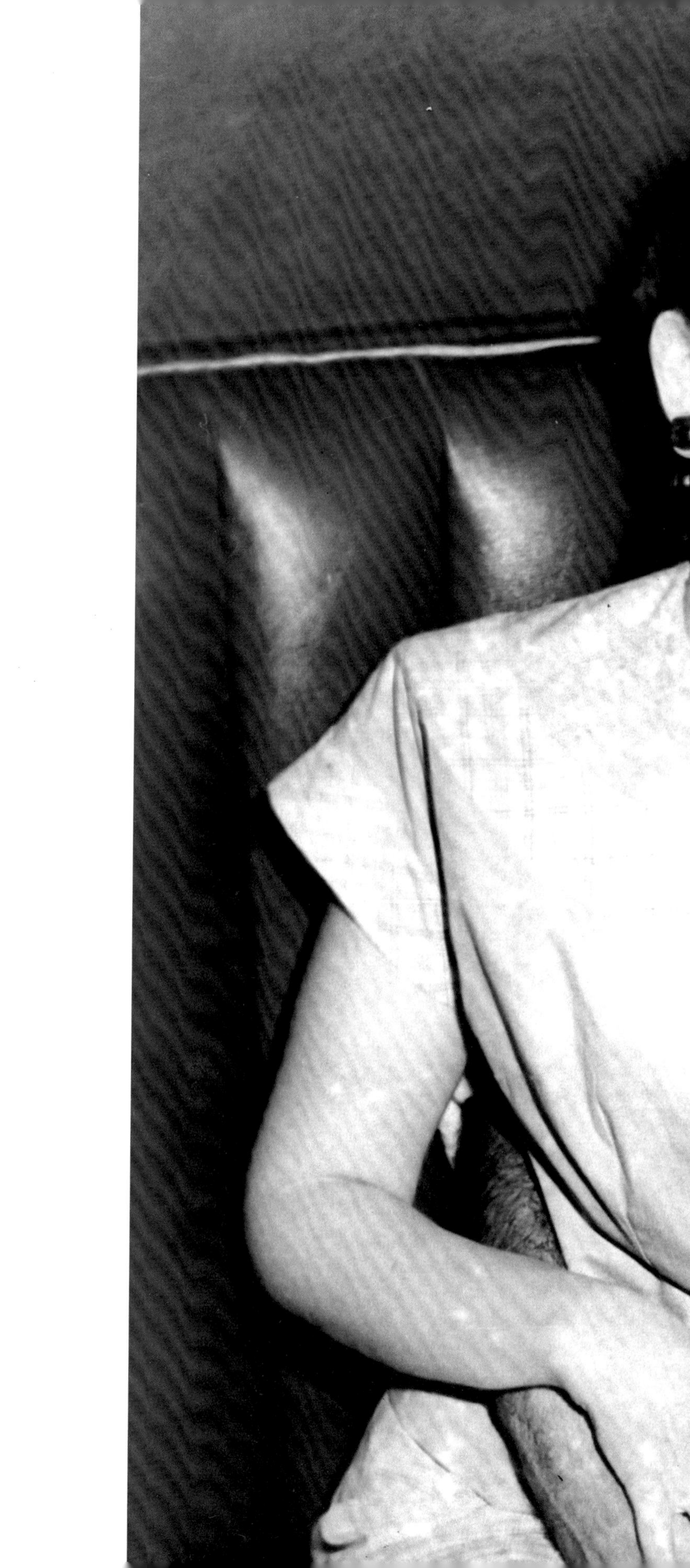

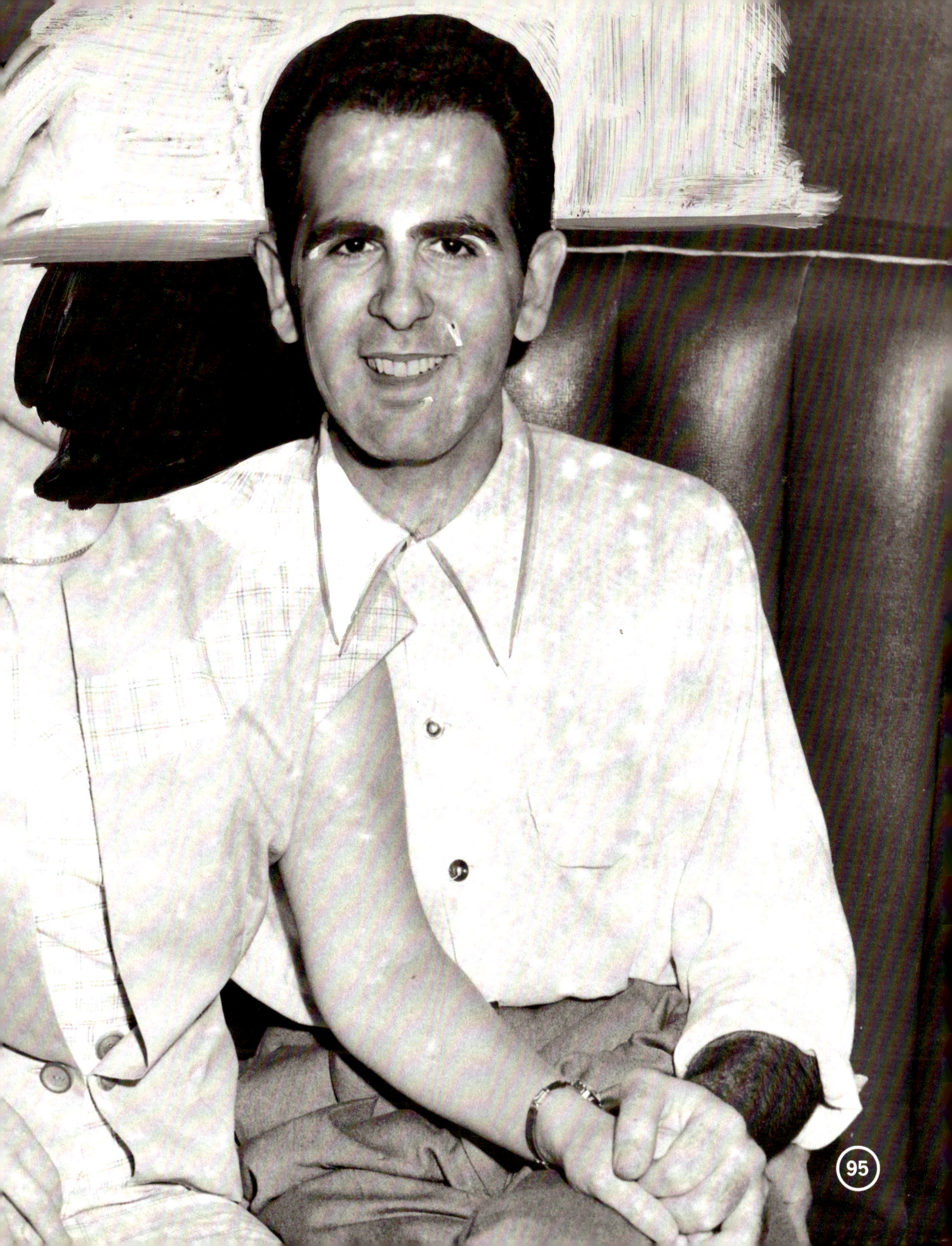

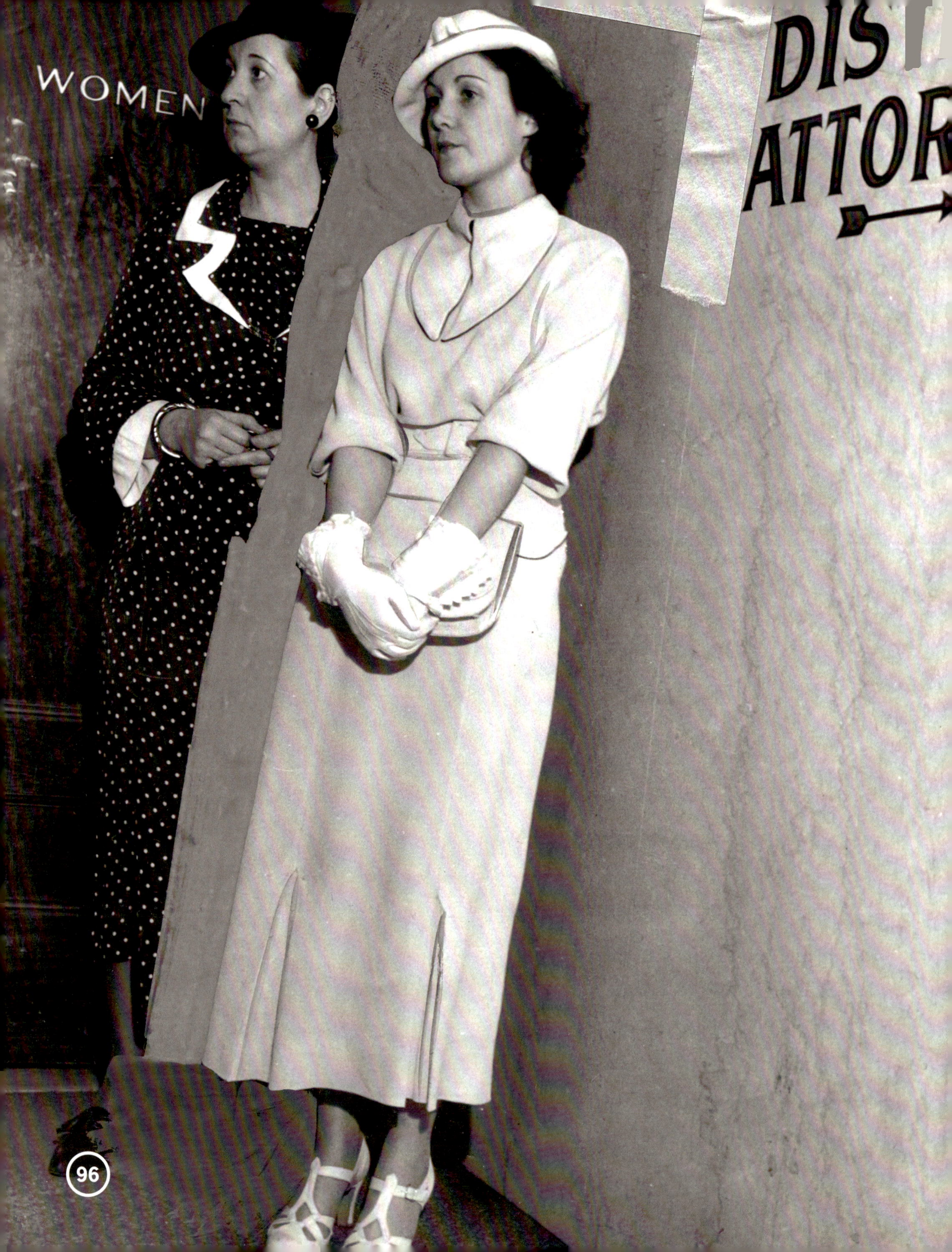

WOMEN
DIS
ATTOR

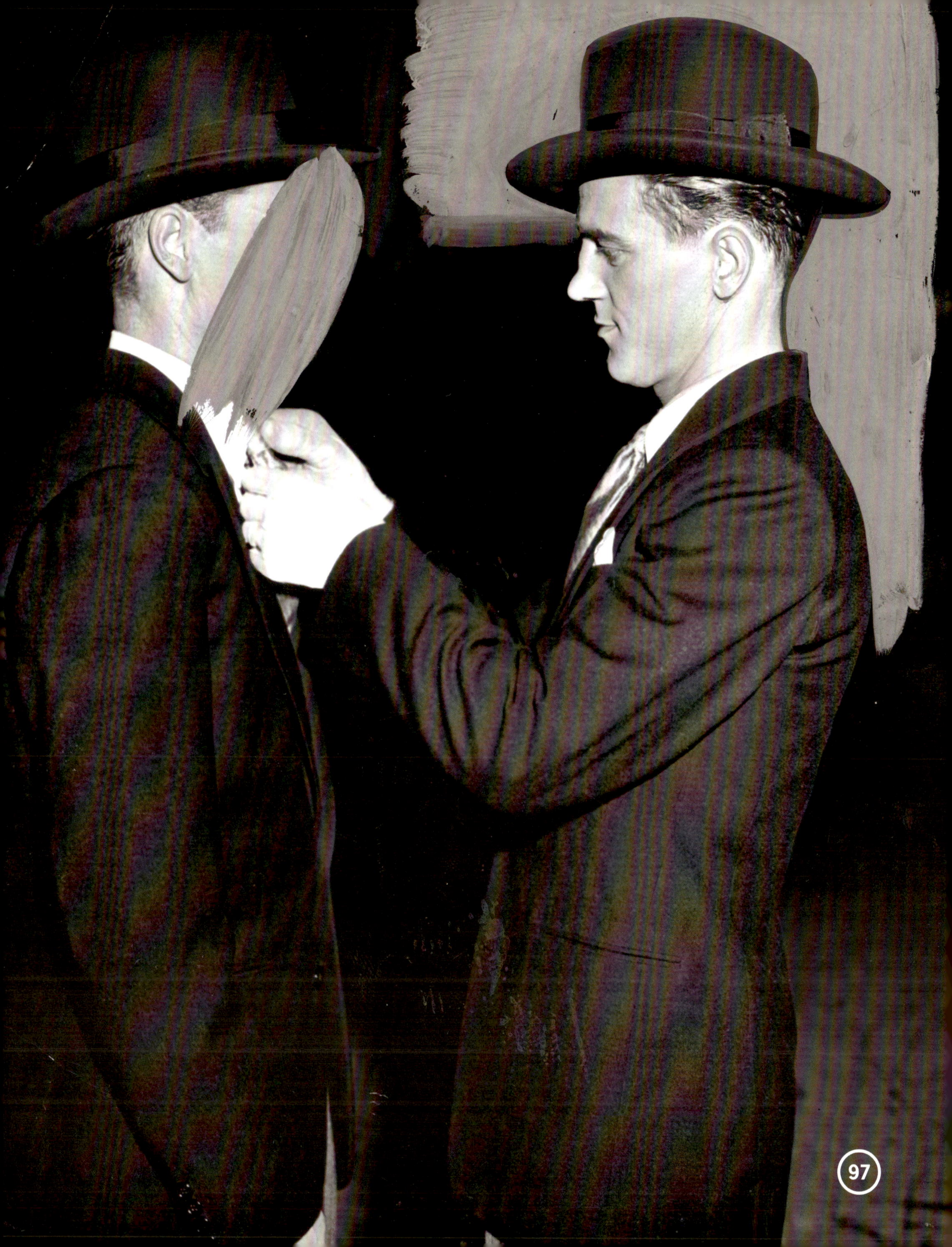

(100) ## JERRY POTTER
OCTOBER 16, 1947 THURSDAY

Christmas mishap brings him $6500

(101) ## VICTIM BEATEN BY BURGLAR
FEBRUARY 11, 1952 MONDAY

MRS. NELL THOMPSON, 62, of **GARDENA**, is treated by **DR. GEORGE ZISLIS** after she was brutally beaten by a burglar in her home. Mrs. Thompson is comforted by a friend, **TONY KREISKI**

(102) ## AS DEATH COMES TO A LITTLE BOY IN THE FISHPOND OF HIS NEW HOME
MAY 22, 1951 TUESDAY

Grief-wracked, with tears running down their cheeks, **MR.** and **MRS. MARCUS SHADDOCK**, standing at left, collapse into each other's arms as **DR. E. H. FOGELBERT** and **FIREMAN R. D.**

ACCIDENTS

WIRICK make futile attempt to revive their son, **TOMMY, 2,** who drowned in backyard fishpond (arrow) of Shaddocks' new residence at **3510 ½ WEST 109TH STREET**. Standing in background is **GARY SHELTON, 6,** who discovered tragedy

(105) ## MOTHER AND SON HURT IN GAS BLAST
NOVEMBER 9, 1948 TUESDAY

Himself swathed in bandages, little **DANIEL SEGAL (RIGHT), 6,** nevertheless kept a vigil today at the hospital bedside of his mother, **MRS. GERTRUDE SEGAL, 36.** Both were burned severely when gas from furnace pilot light exploded in home at **1936 NORTH CARMEN AVENUE, HOLLYWOOD**

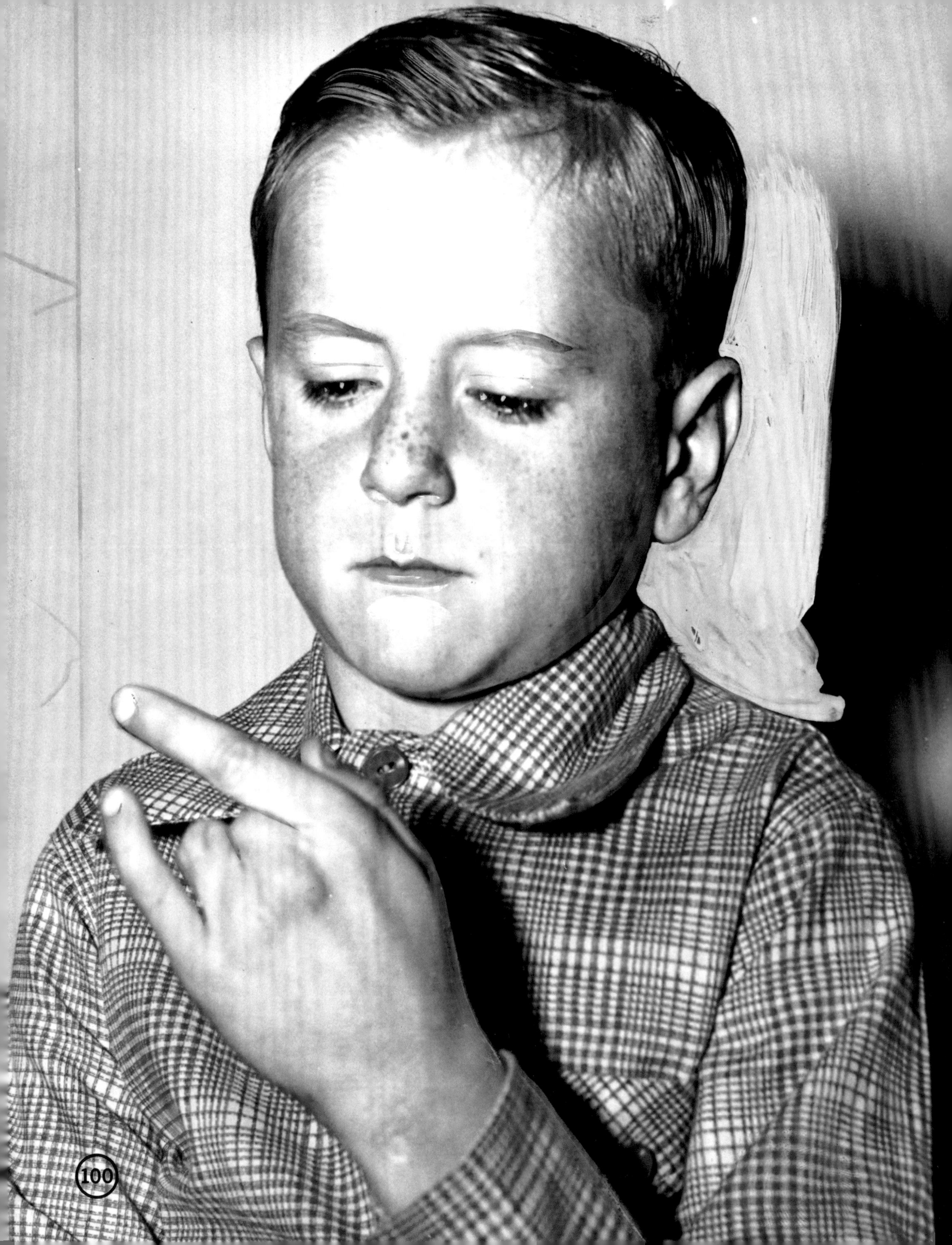
100

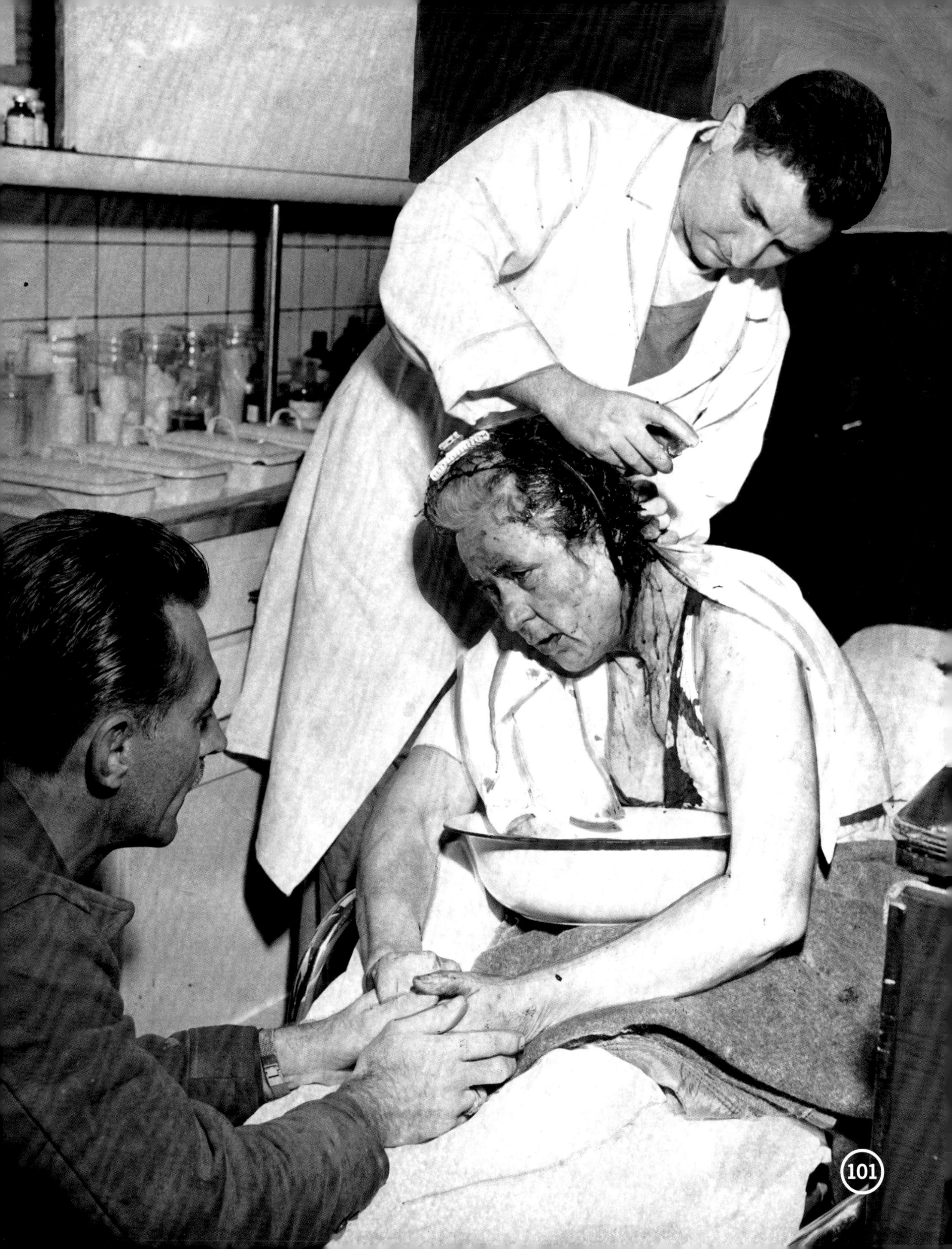

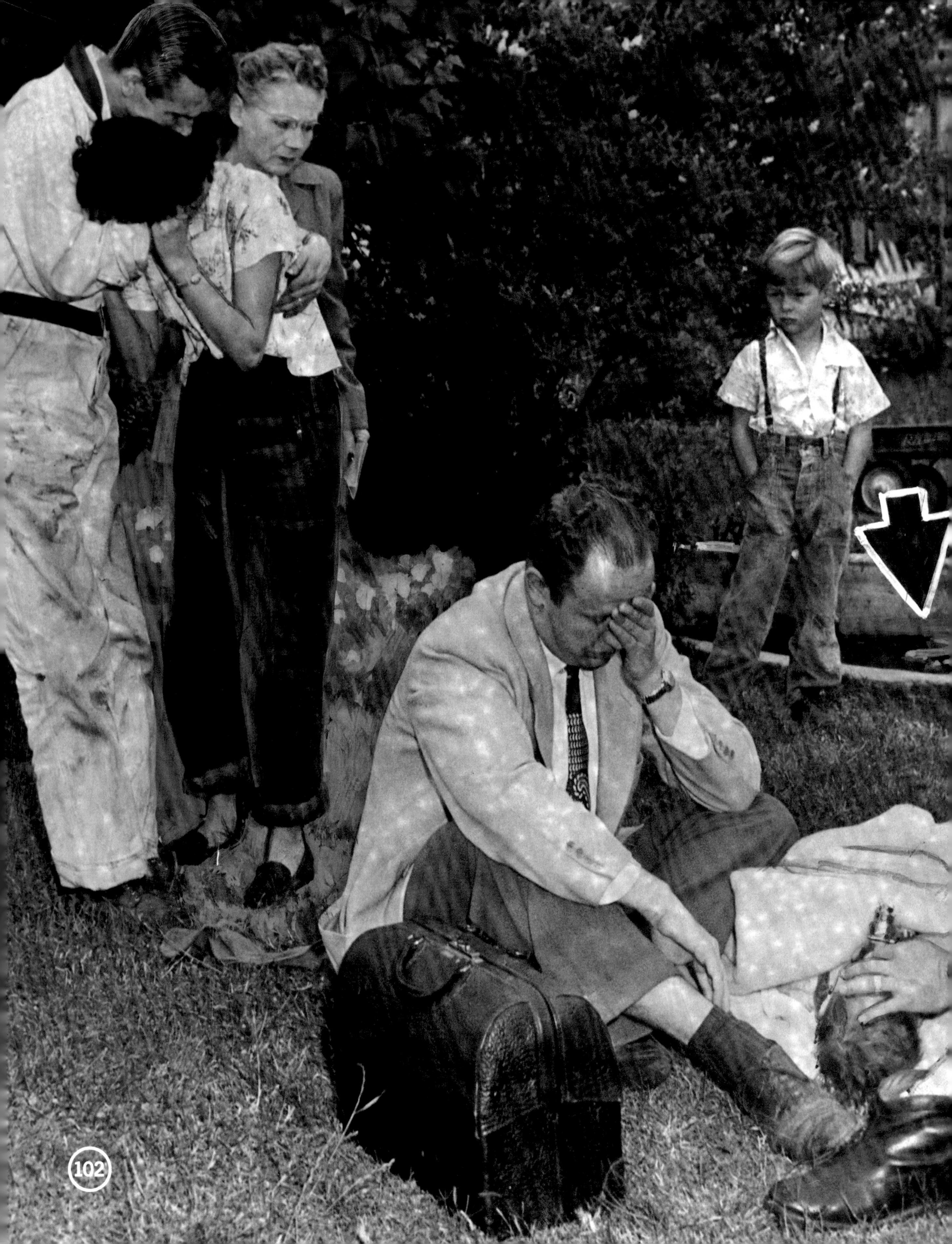

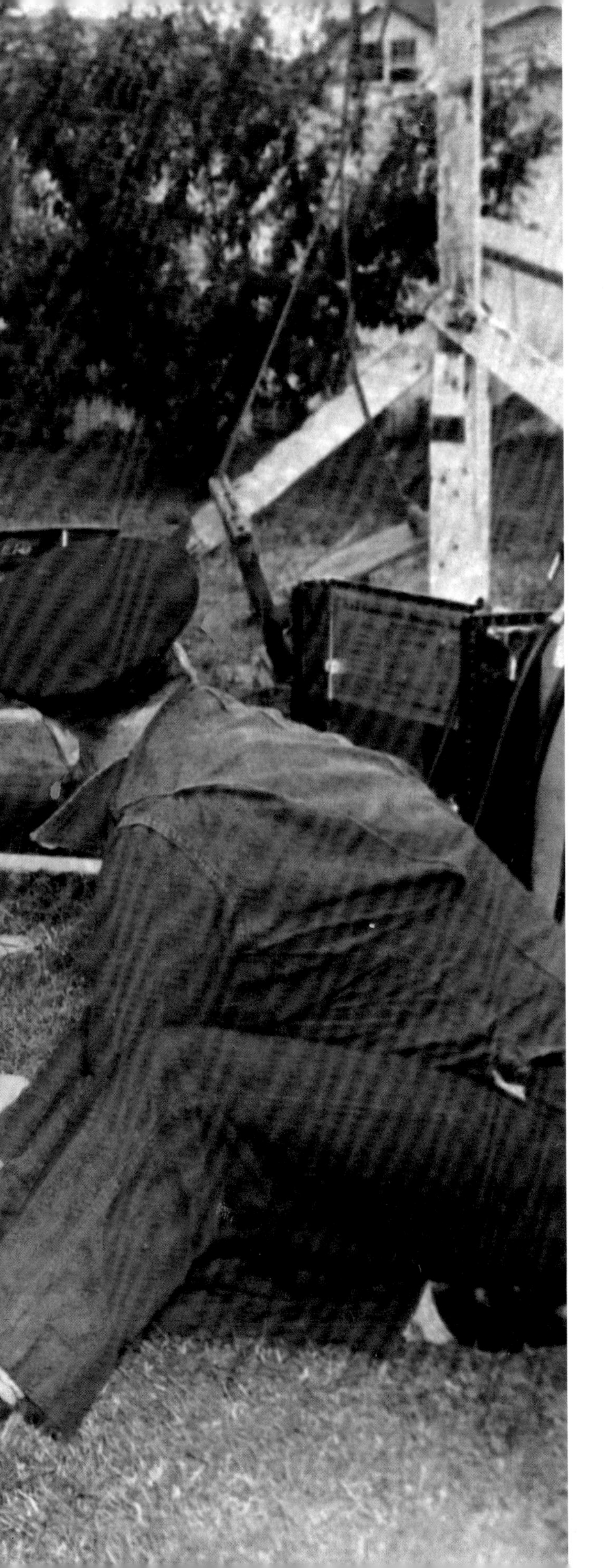

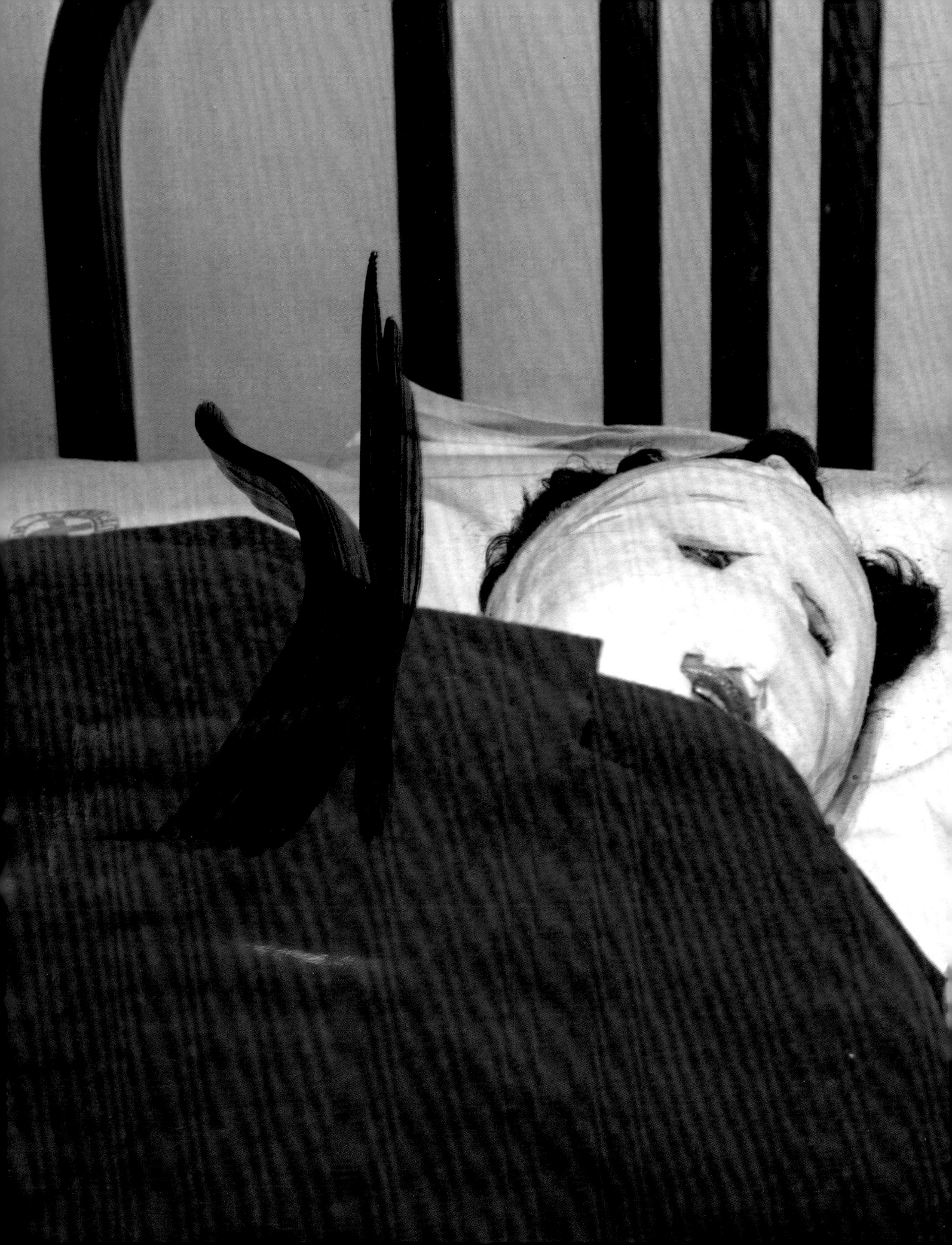

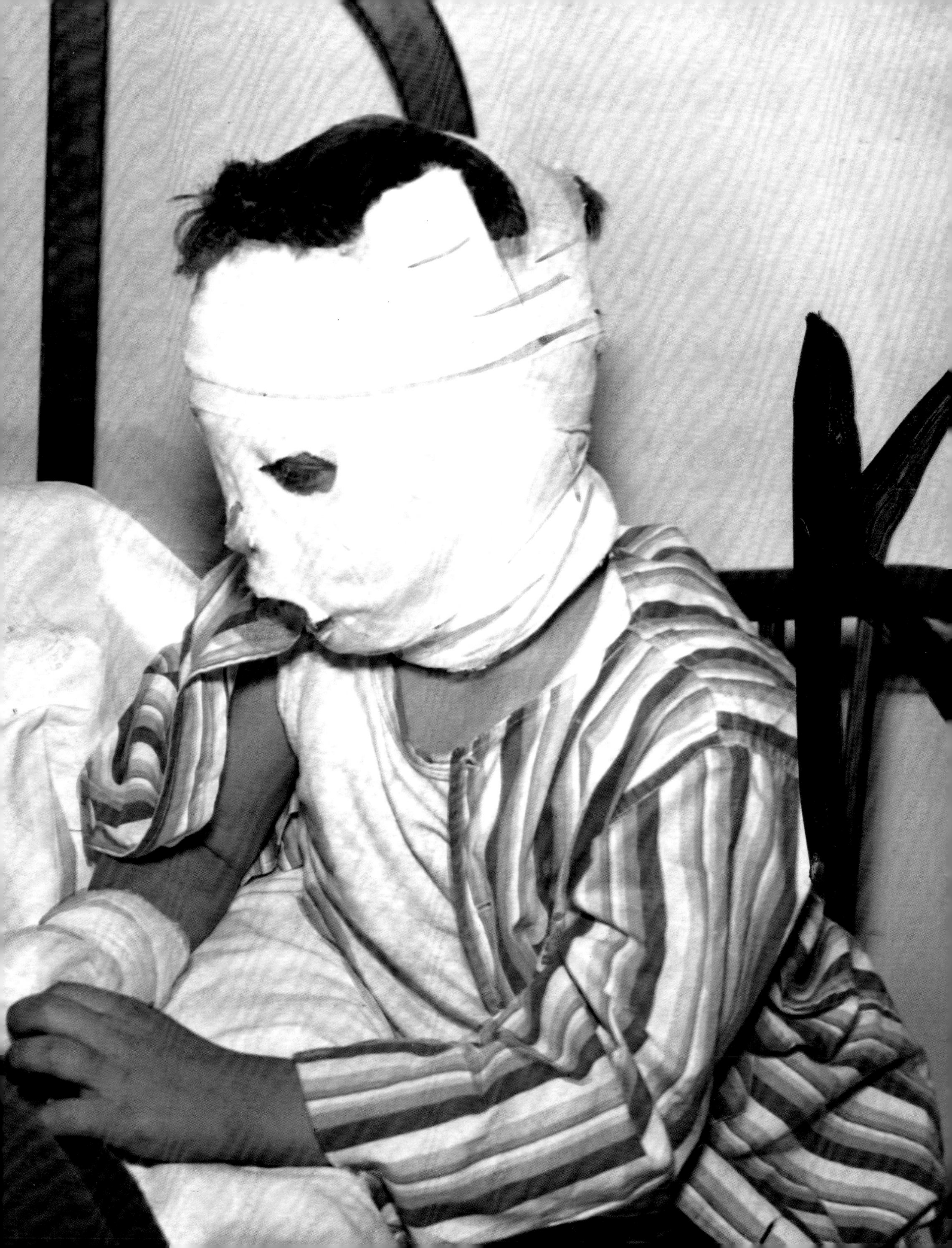

CROSS-

DRESSERS

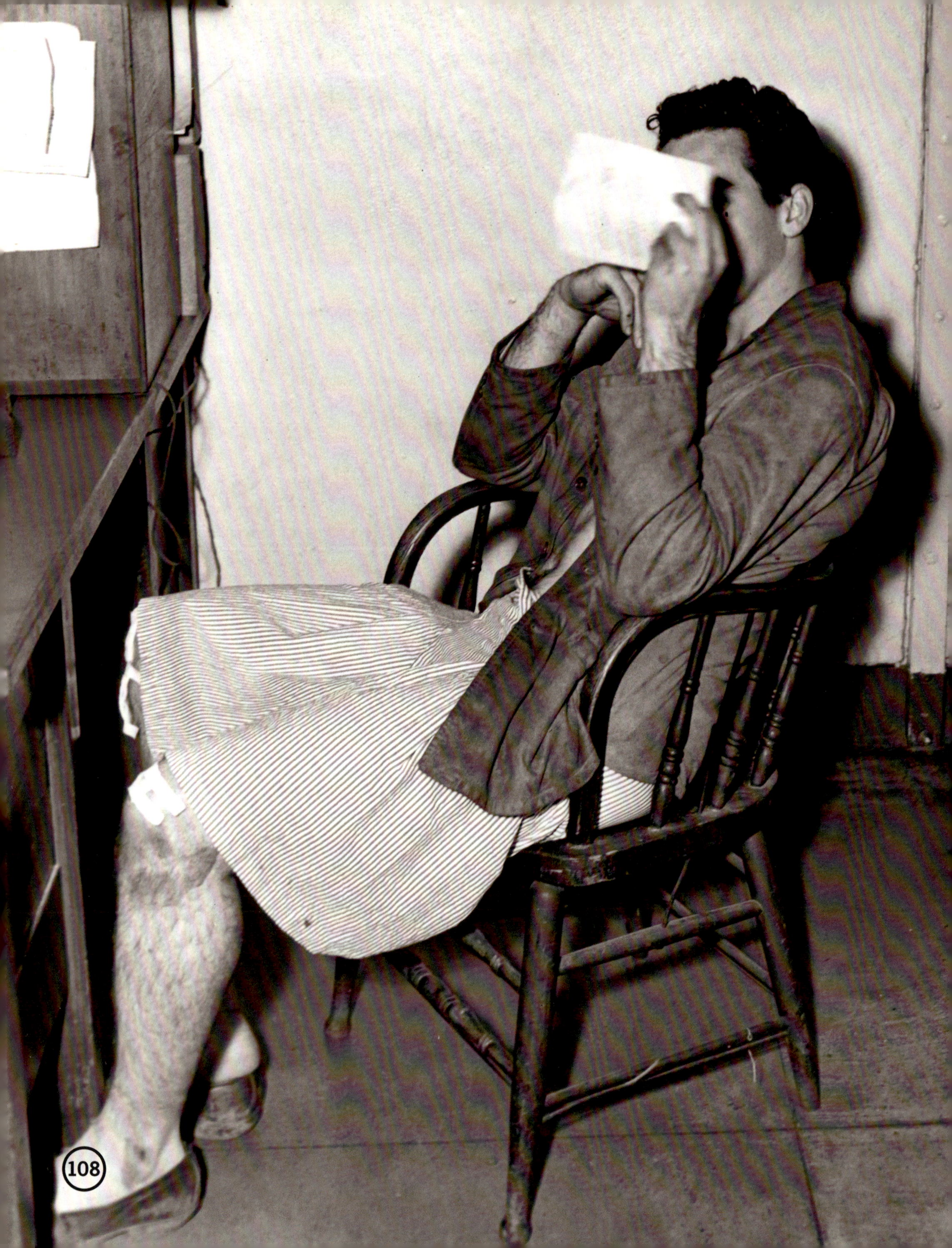

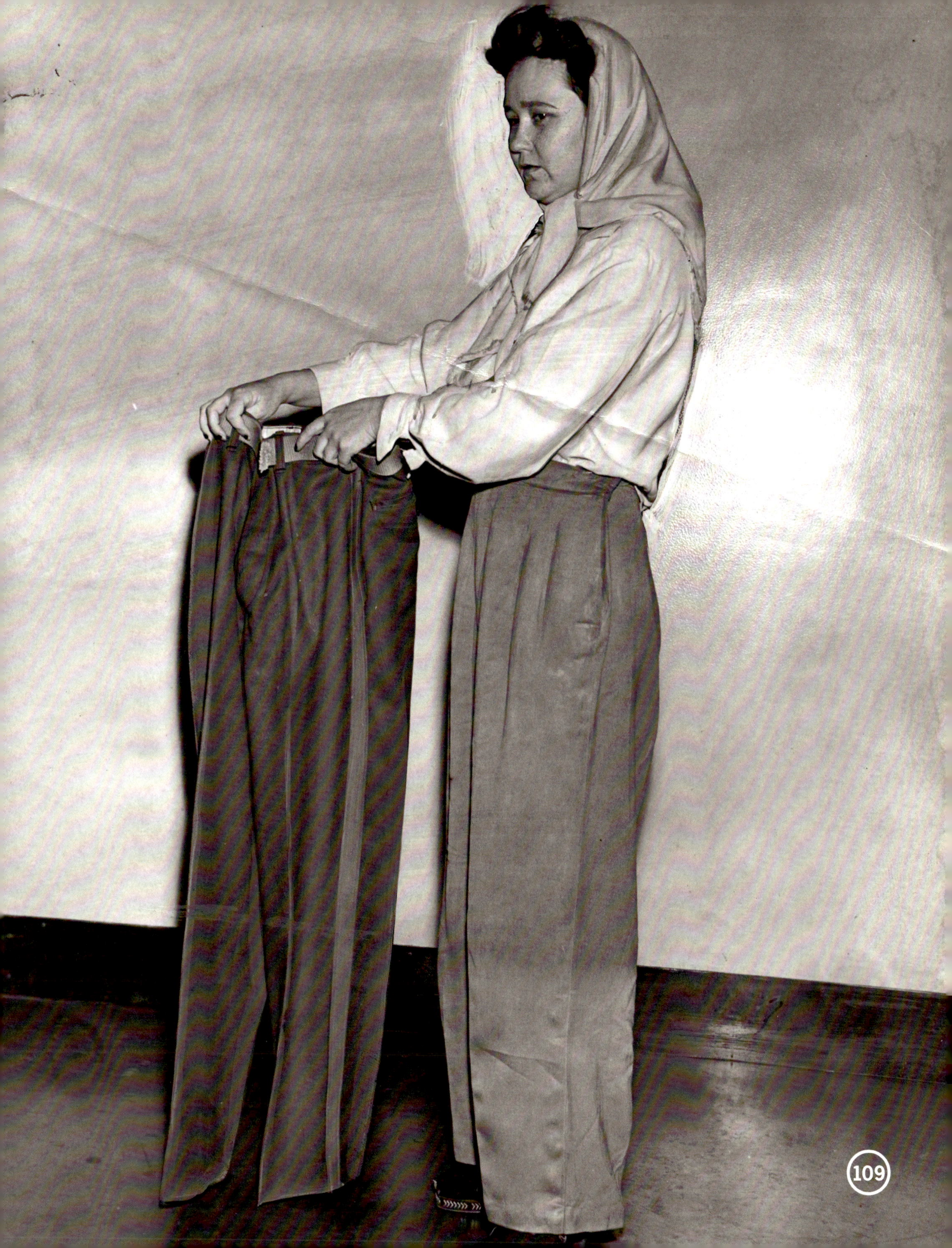

109

Bodies of **ALVIN ROBERTS** and his wife, **MAXINE**, lie in friend's Hollywood apartment after Roberts pumped three bullets into wife's body, then shot himself through head. Dual tragedy followed family quarrel

Body of **BERT WILLIAMS**, **61**, who had been missing from his home since Saturday, is shown where it was found today,

SLAIN

beside the main line right-of-way of **SOUTHERN PACIFIC RAILROAD**, near **LINCOLN HEIGHTS JAIL.** Examining it are, left to right, **GILL LAURES** of police department; **ROBERT CARVER**, who found the body, and **DETECTIVE R. D. CAMPBELL**

MRS. MAY LORENA PRESTON, strangled to death and dumped out $\frac{1}{4}$ mile south of **CENTER STREET** and the **SAN GABRIEL RIVER** in **NORWALK**

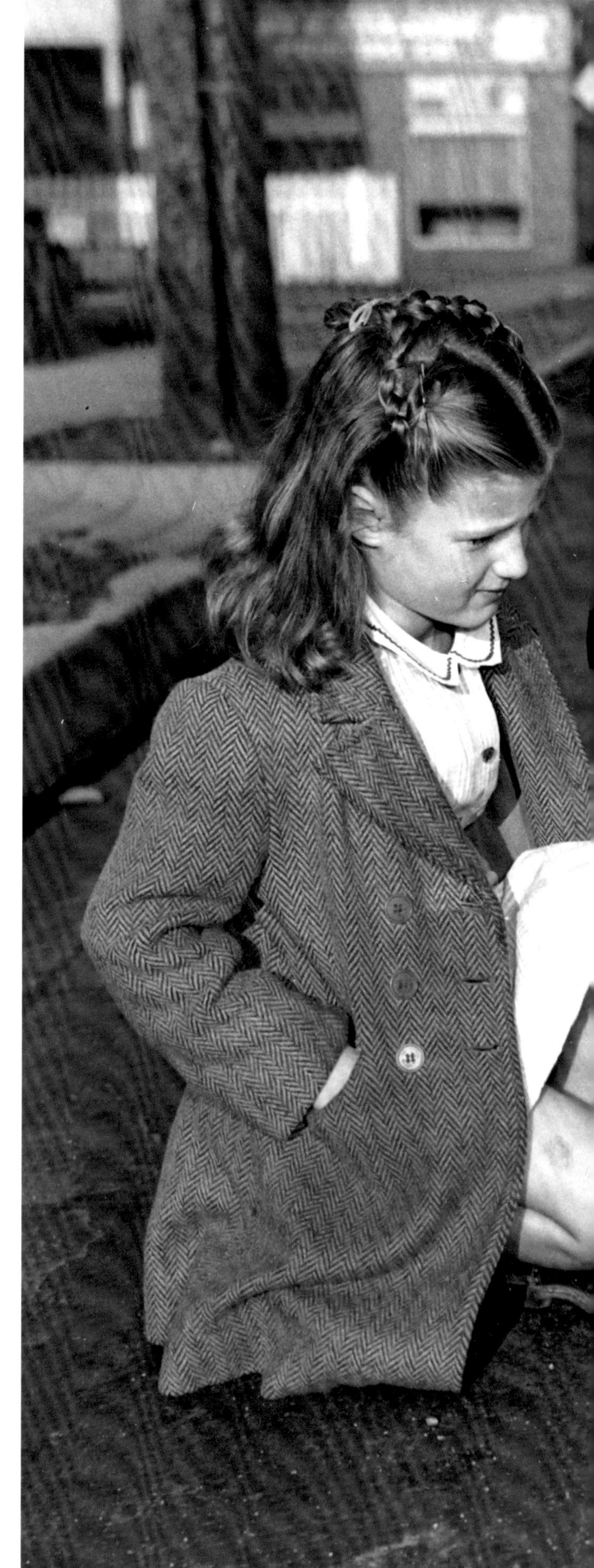

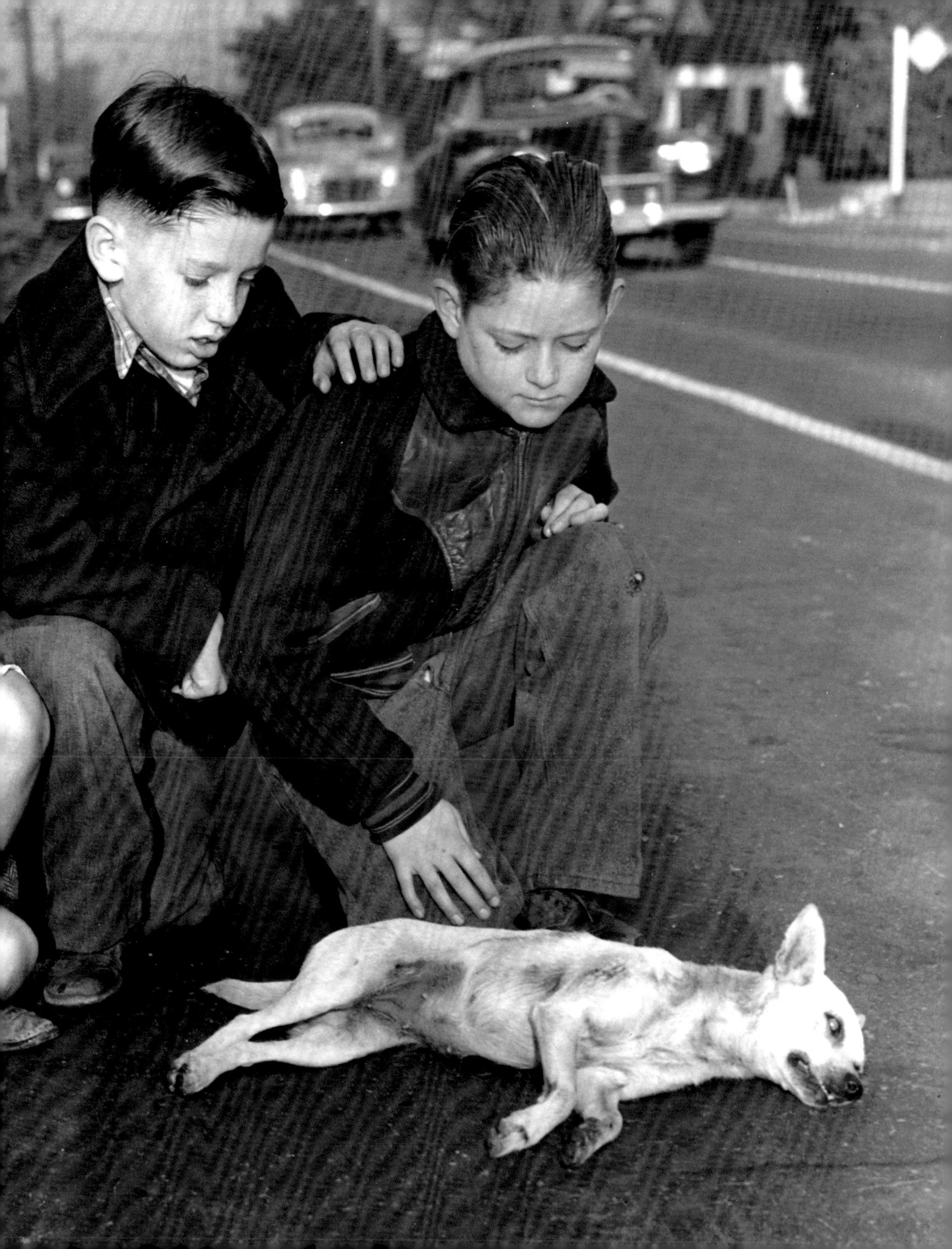

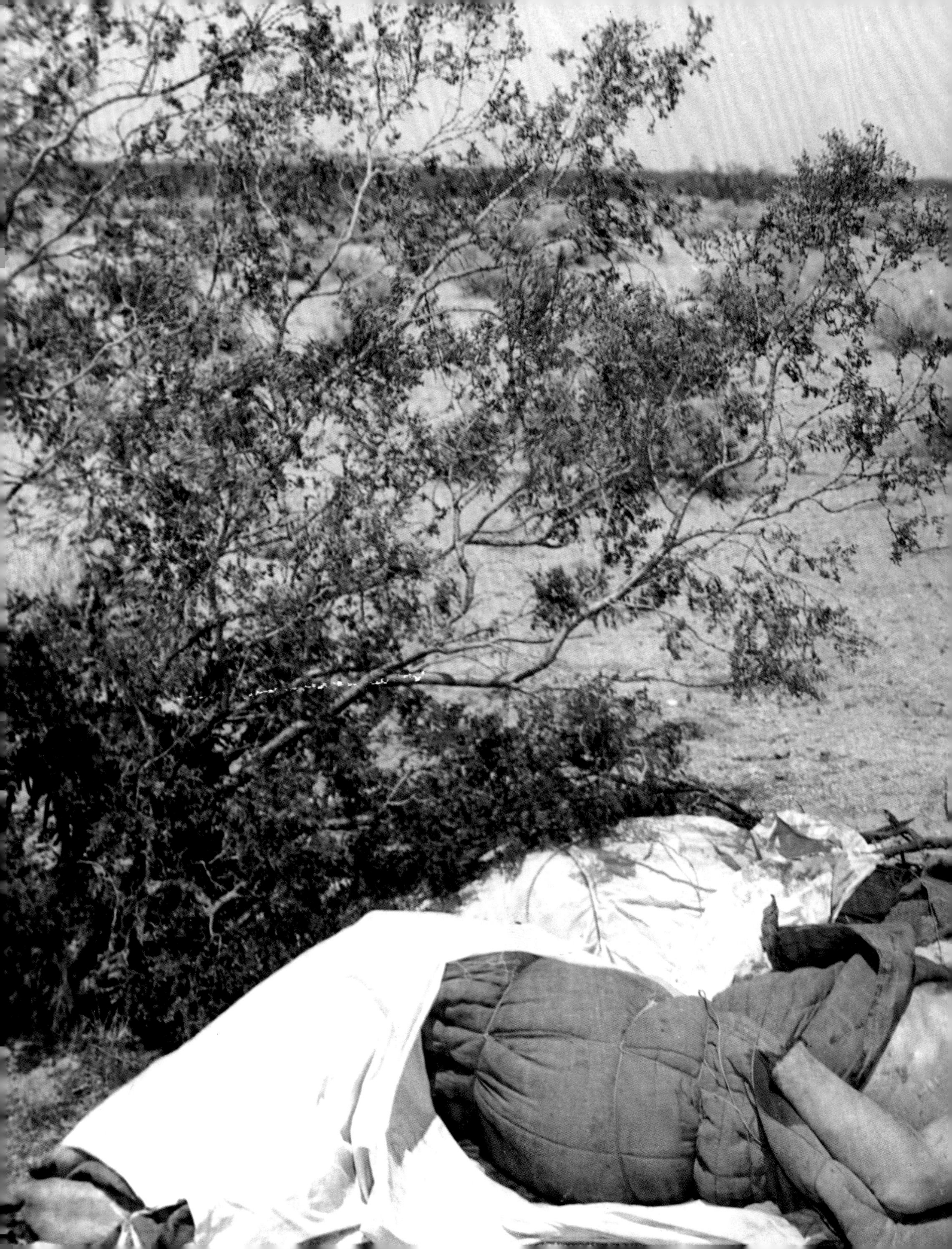

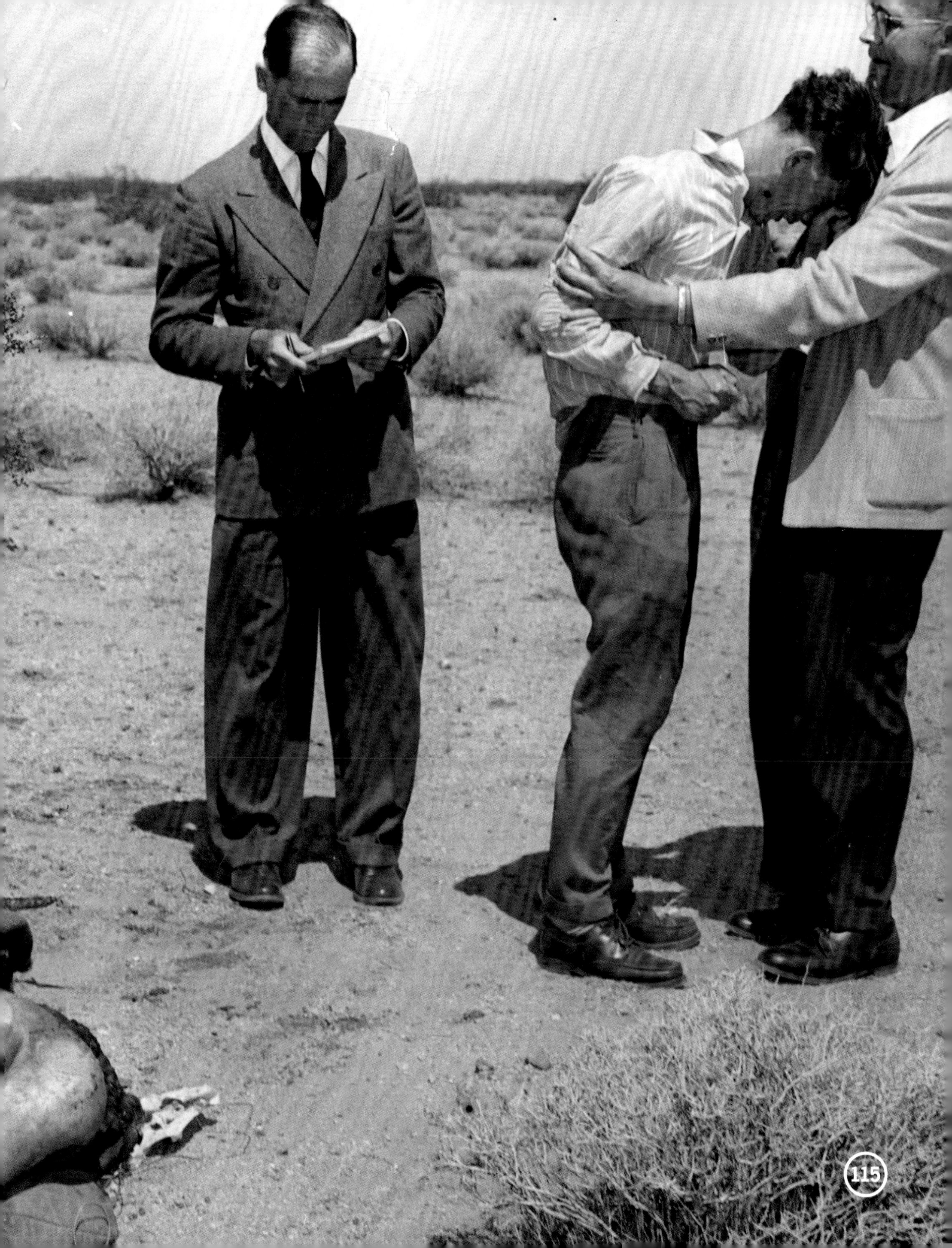

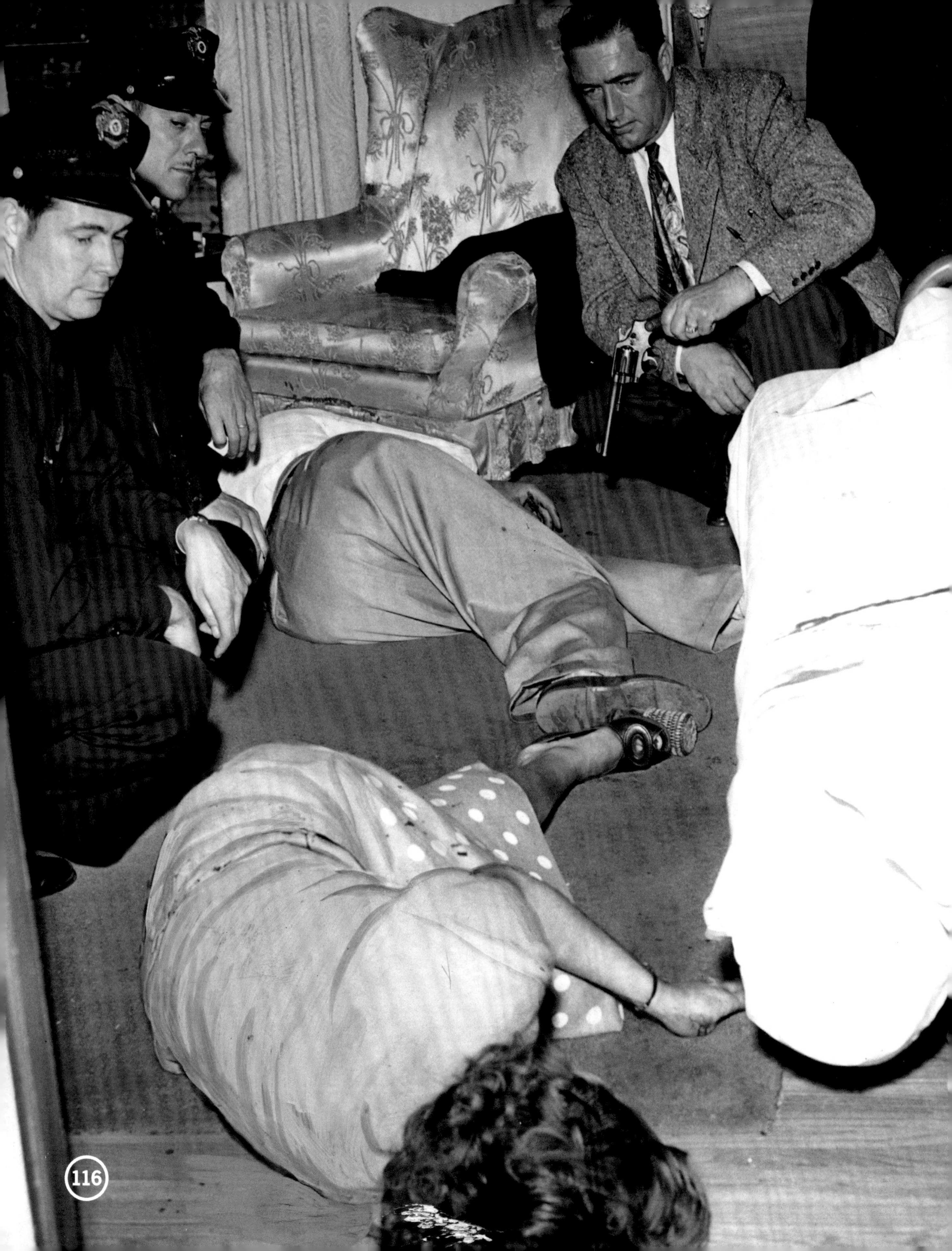

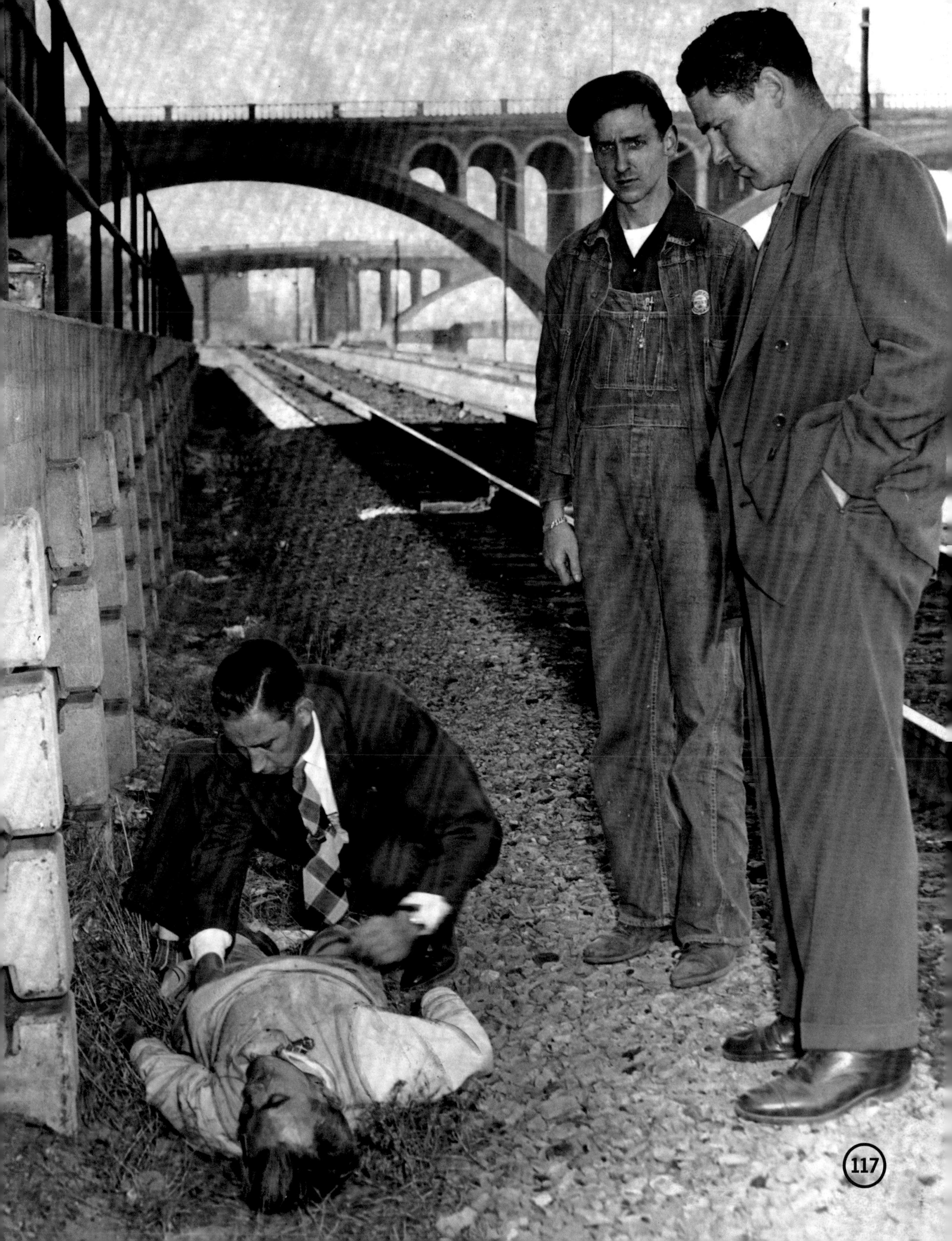

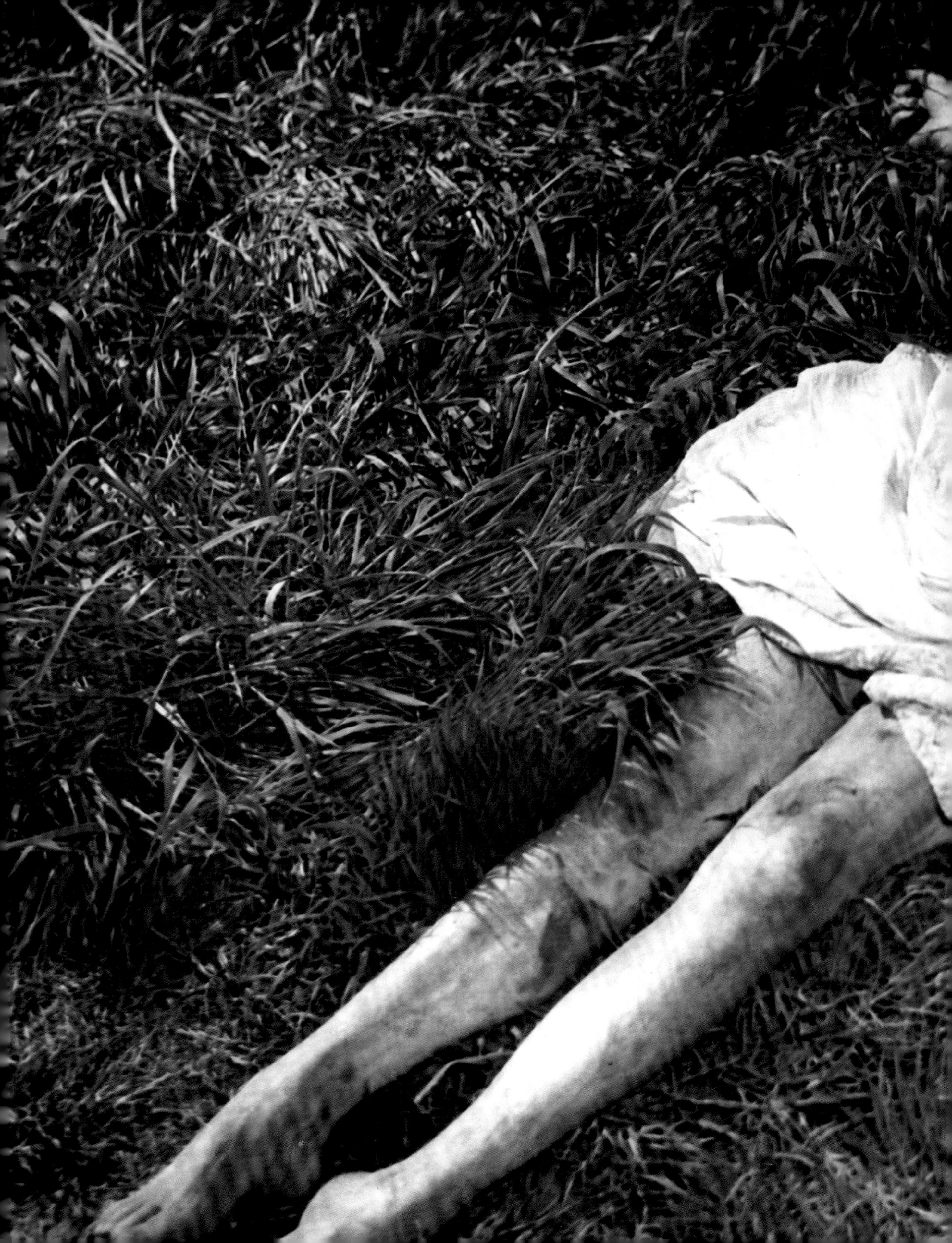

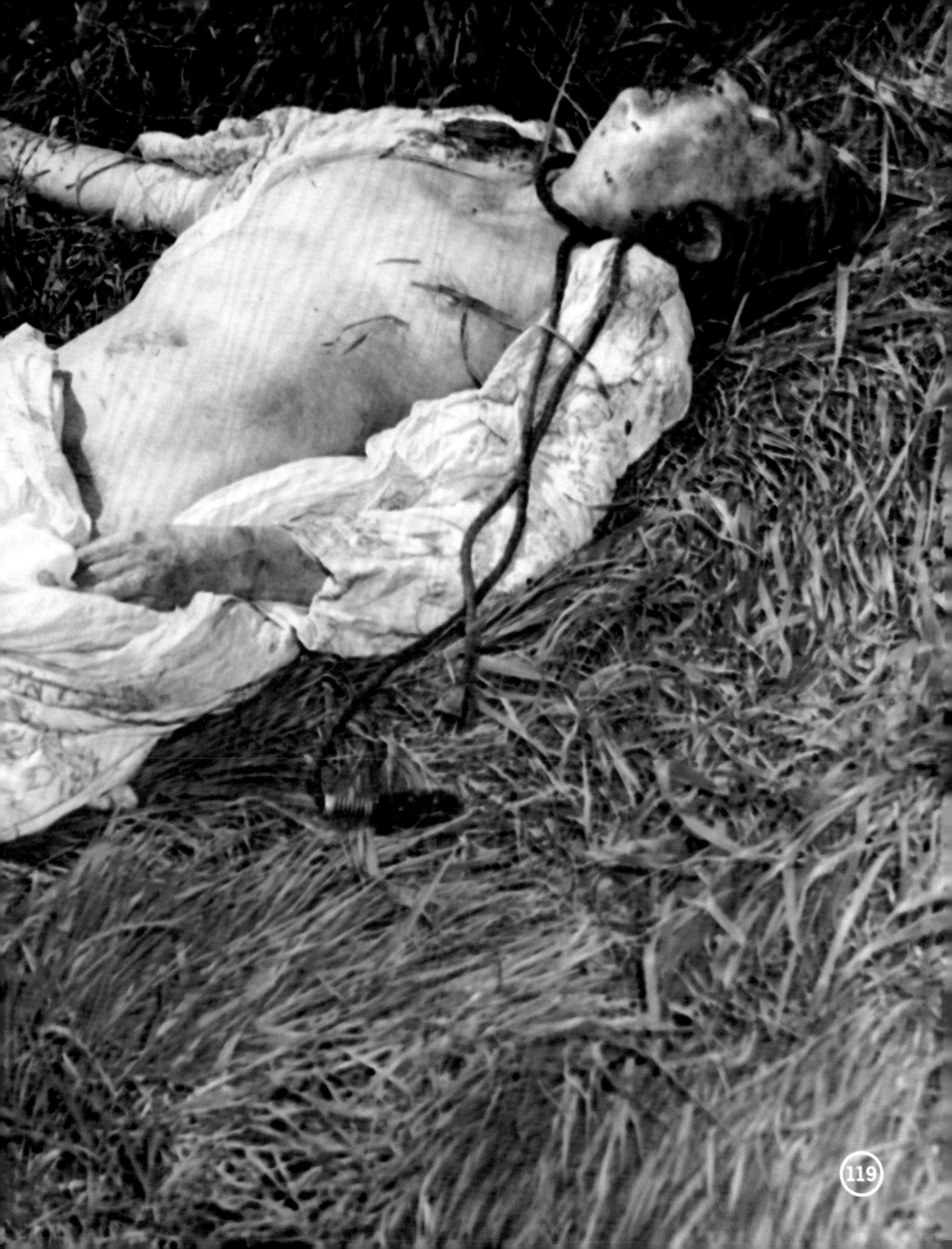

COMMUNITY

ACTIVITIES

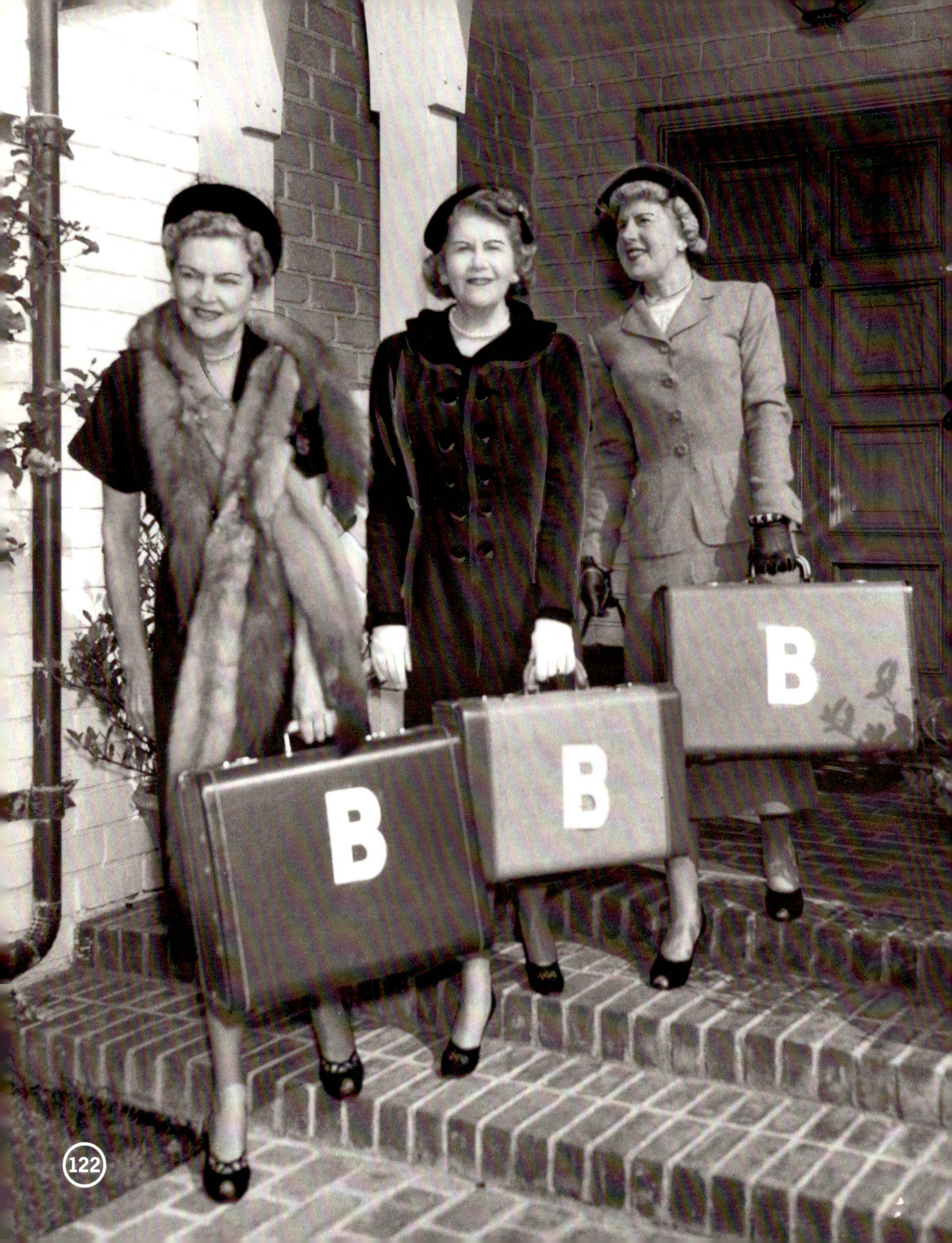

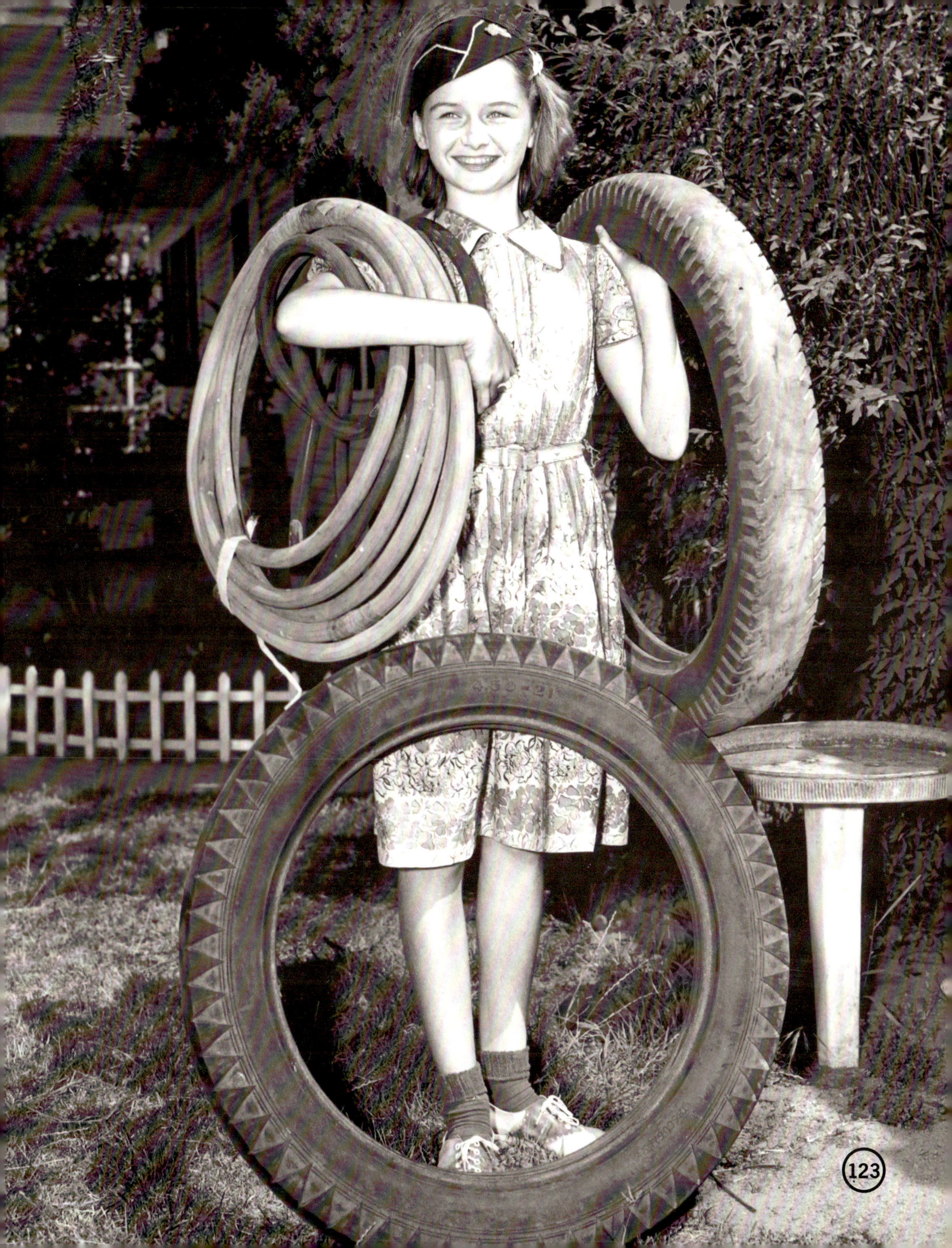

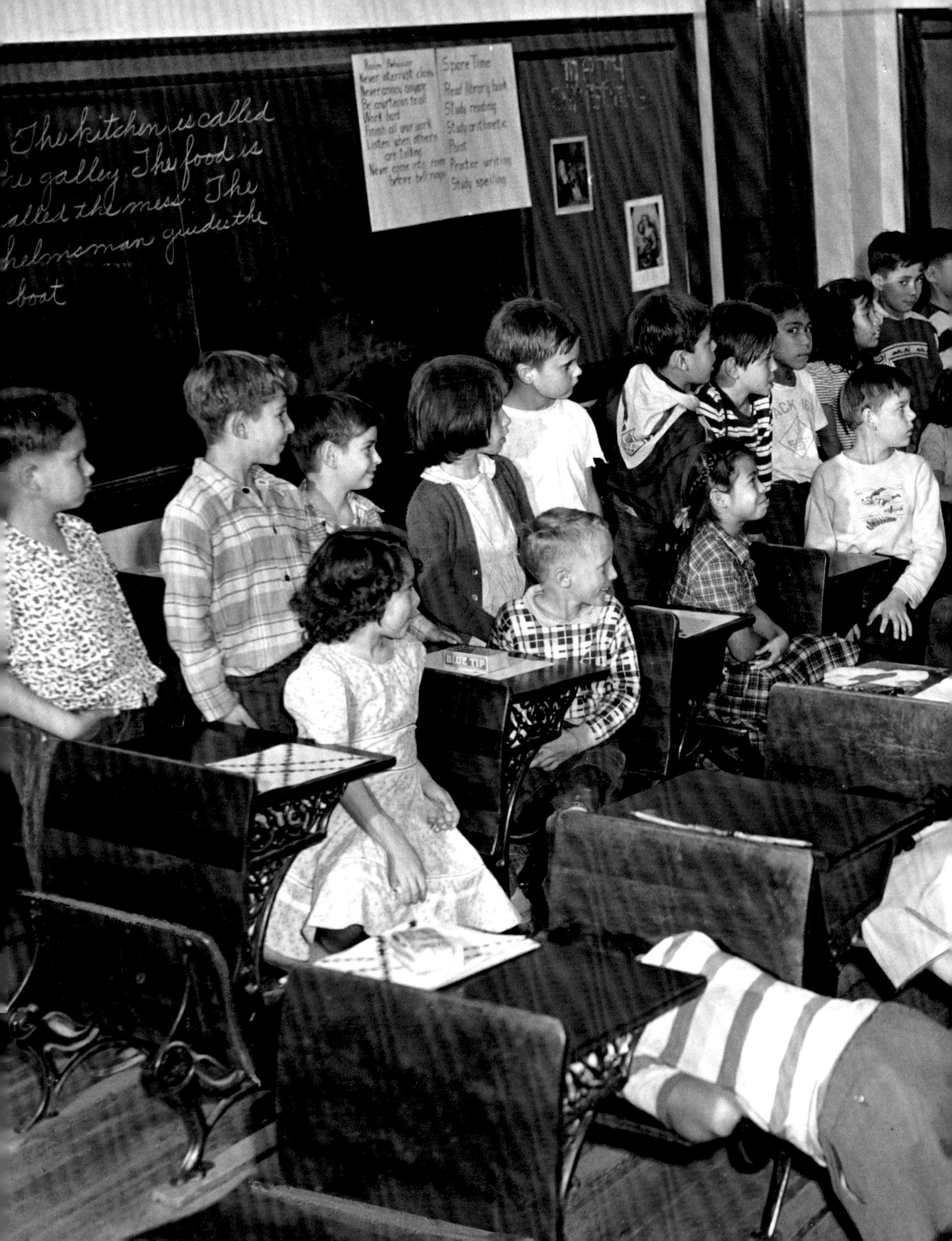

The kitchen is called the galley. The food is called the mess. The helmsman guides the boat
Room Behavior
Never interrupt class
Never annoy anyone
Be courteous to all
Work hard
Finish all your work
Listen when others are talking
Never come into room before bell rings
Spare Time
Read library book
Study reading
Study arithmetic
Paint
Practice writing
Study spelling

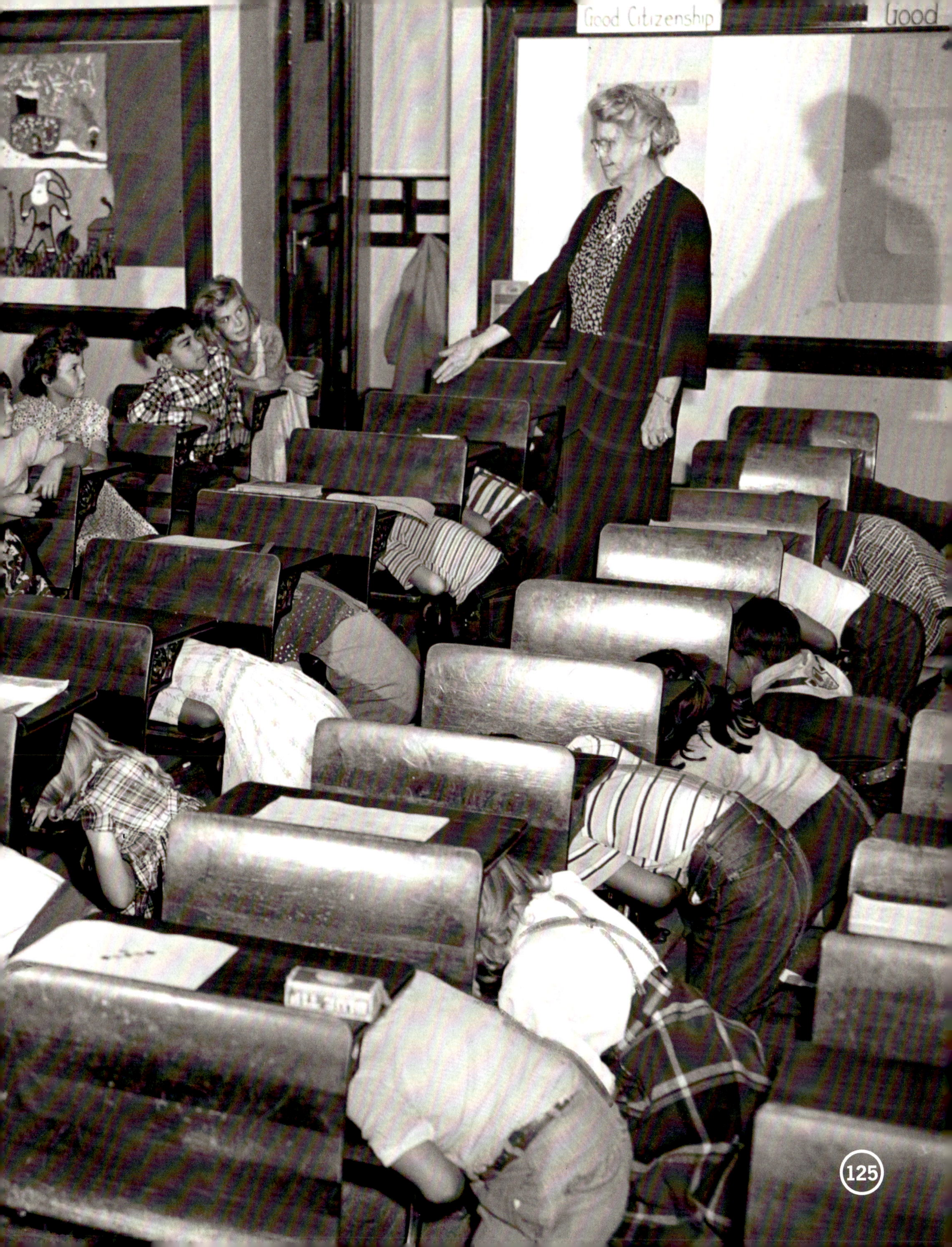

Good Citizenship
Good

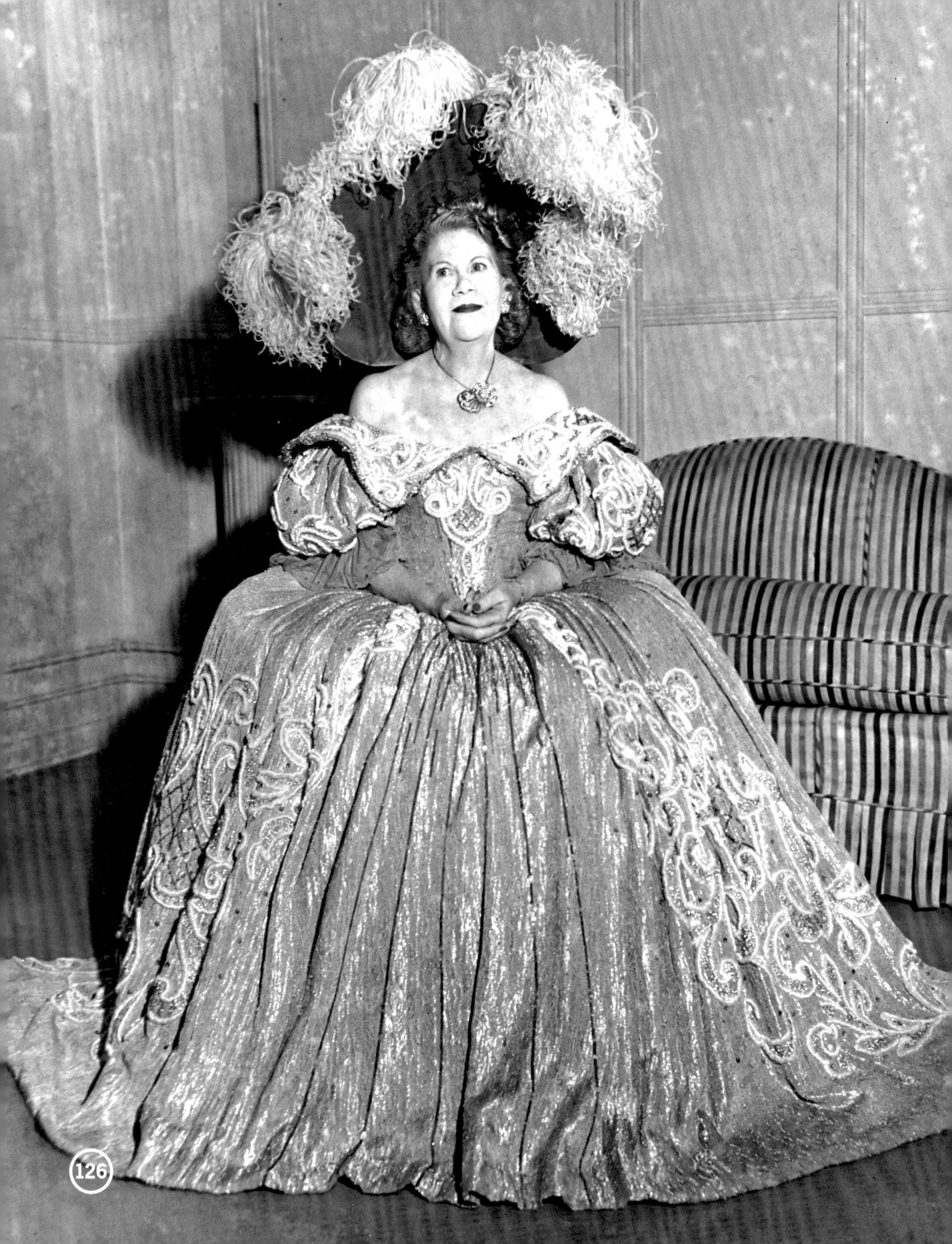

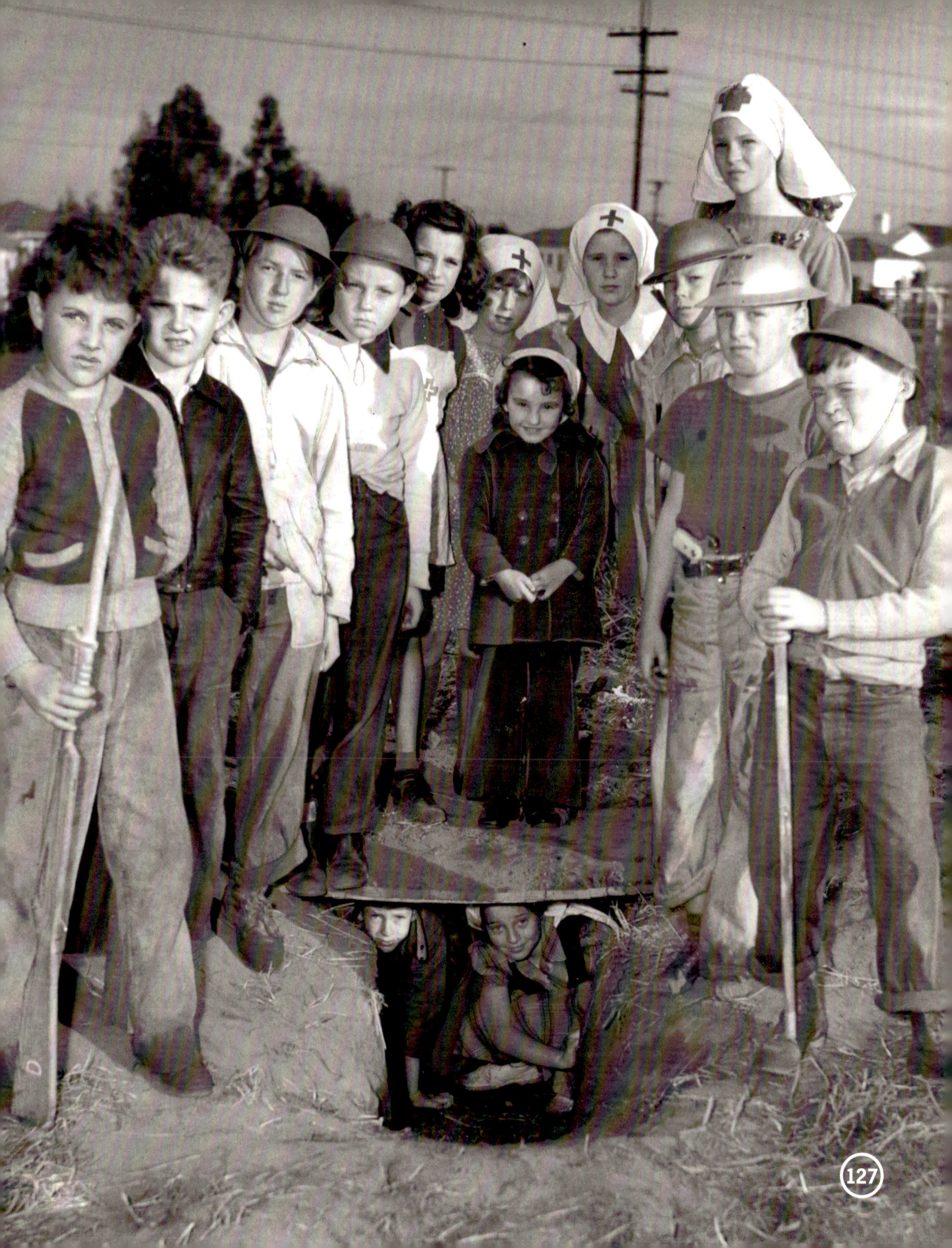

MOVIE STUDIO GOES UP IN FLAMES IN A NIGHT OF STORM TERROR
JANUARY 16, 1952 WEDNESDAY

Blaze rages through **FRONTIER PICTURES CO. STUDIO** at **1357 GORDON STREET.** Ten fire companies finally brought flames under control, but not until the blaze had caused damage estimated at $200,000

FAMILY SUFFERED BURNS IN TRAILER BLAST
DATE UNKNOWN

Couple and their baby were burned seriously when butane gas exploded in this trailer at **FIRESTONE PARK**

DISASTERS

FLOOD OR NO FLOOD, CHILDREN MUST PLAY
JULY 20, 1951 FRIDAY

TOMMY GODFREY, 4, rides his tricycle in water in front of his flooded home at **1732 ELDORADO STREET,** as his mother, **PAULINE,** stands by

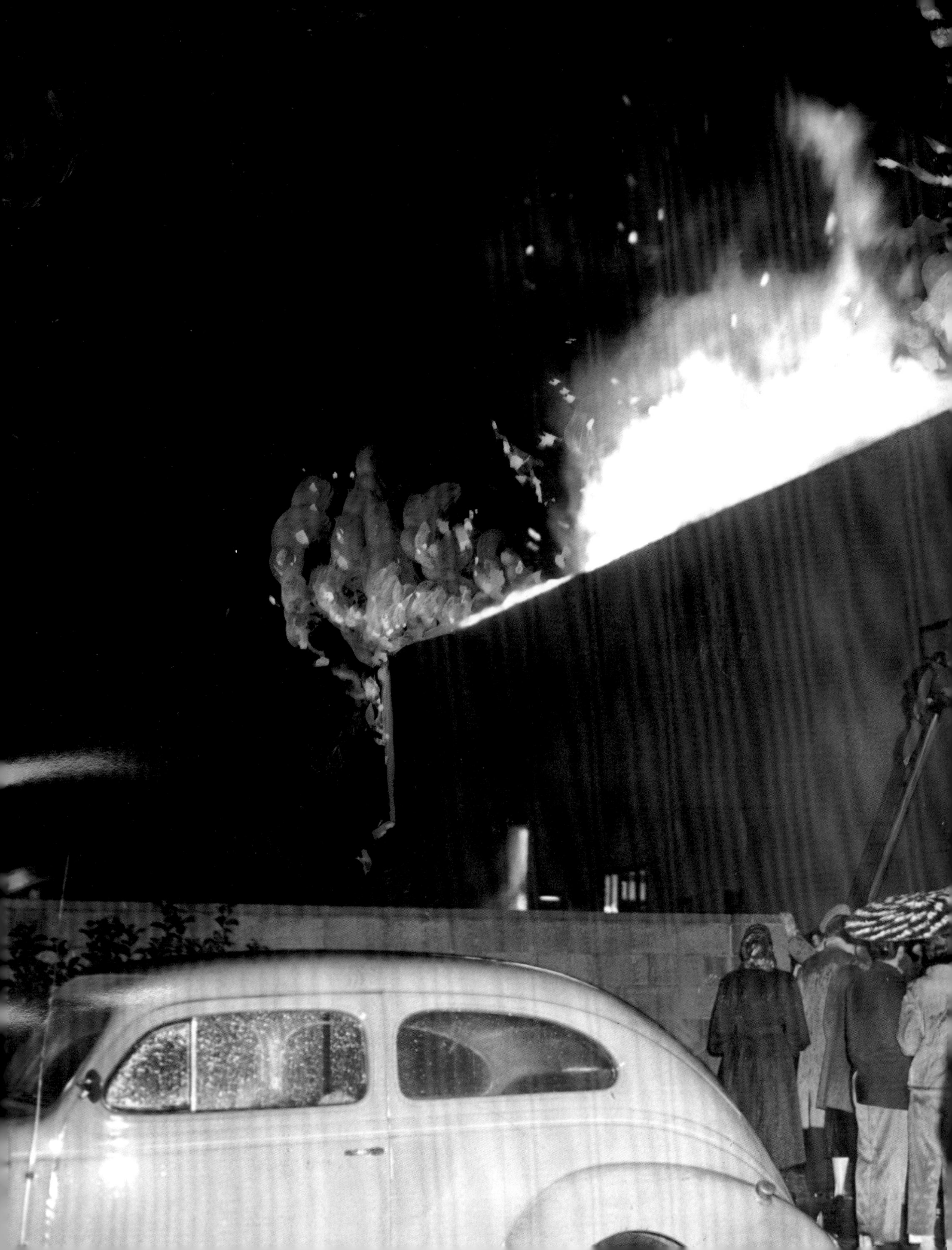

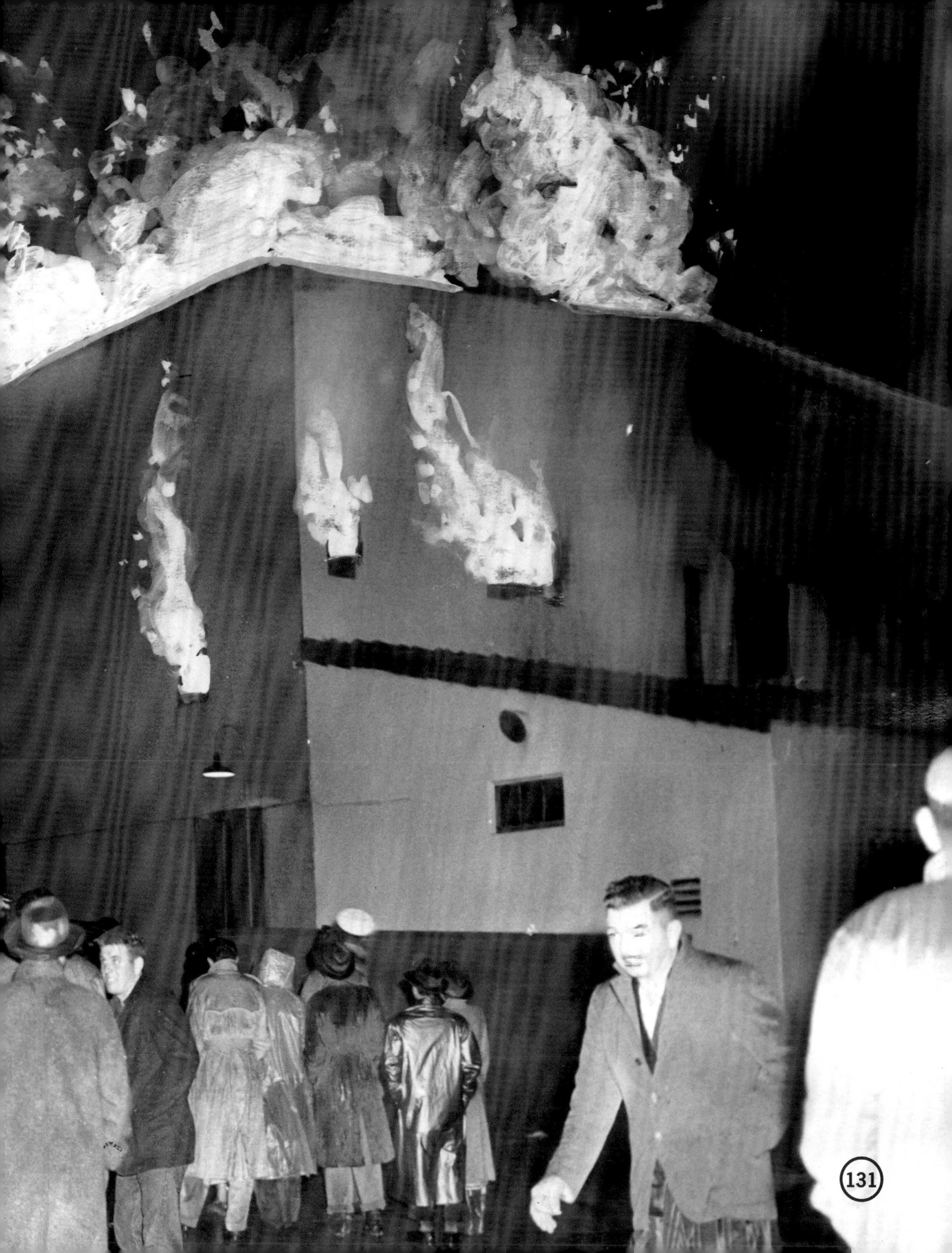

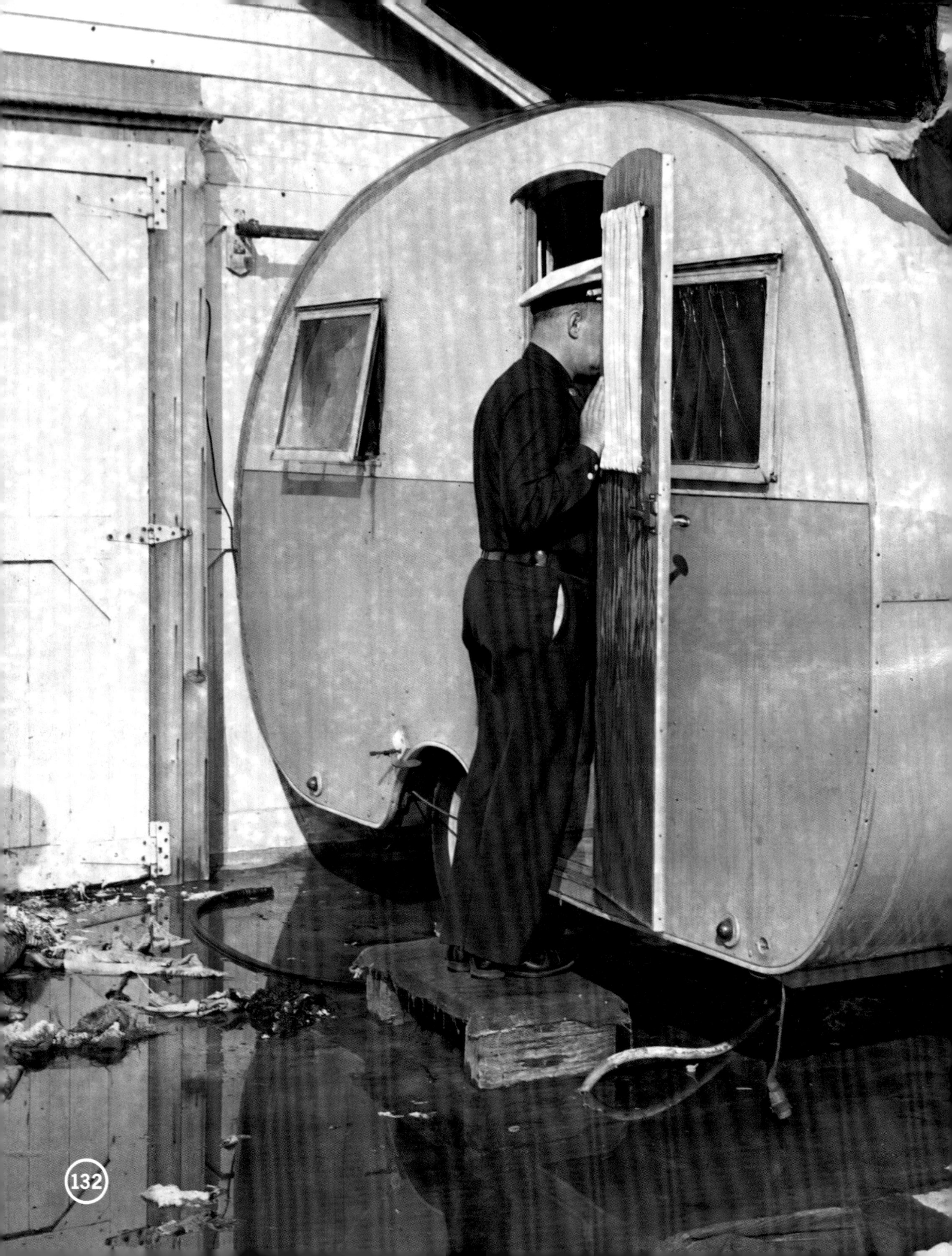

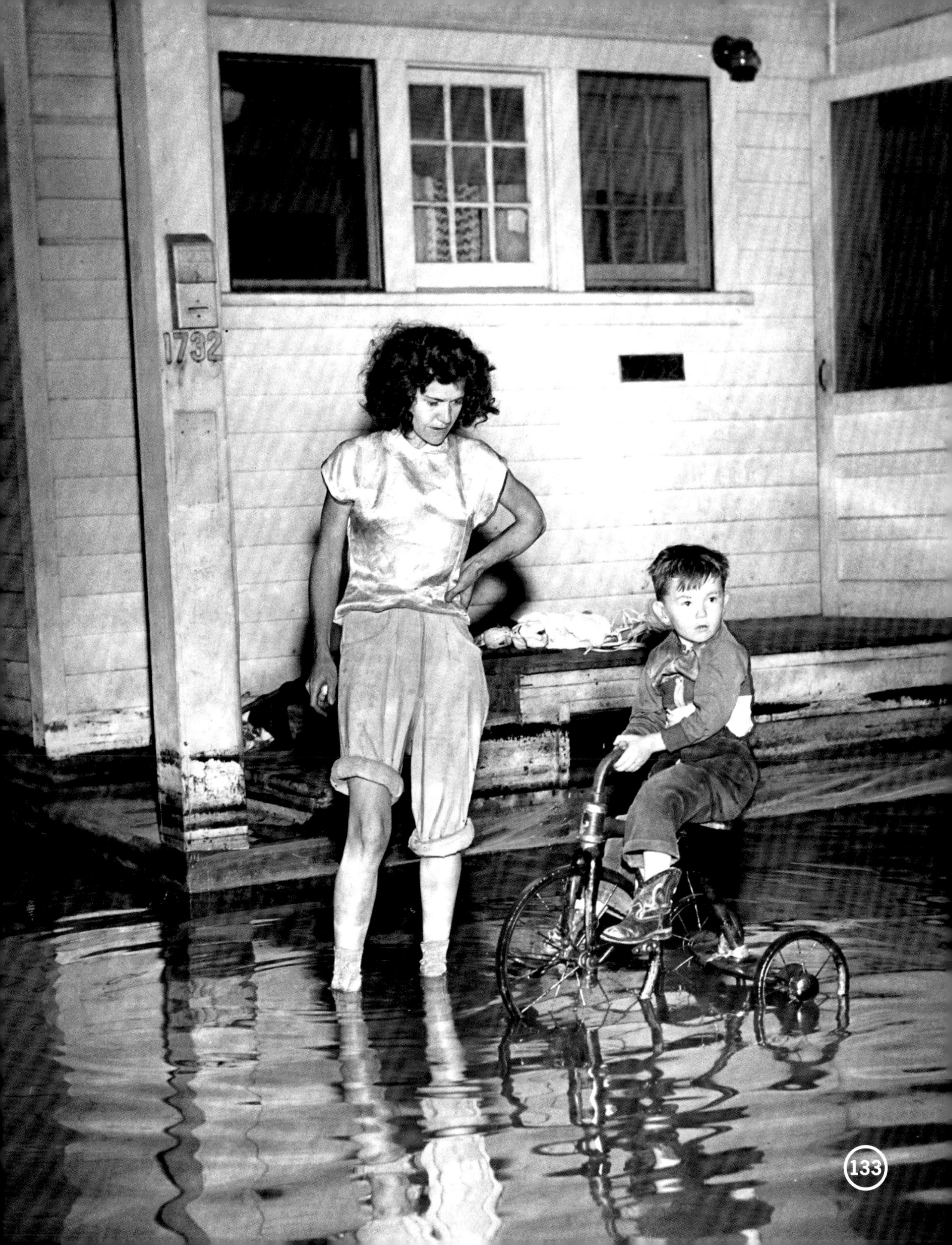

1732

FOUND

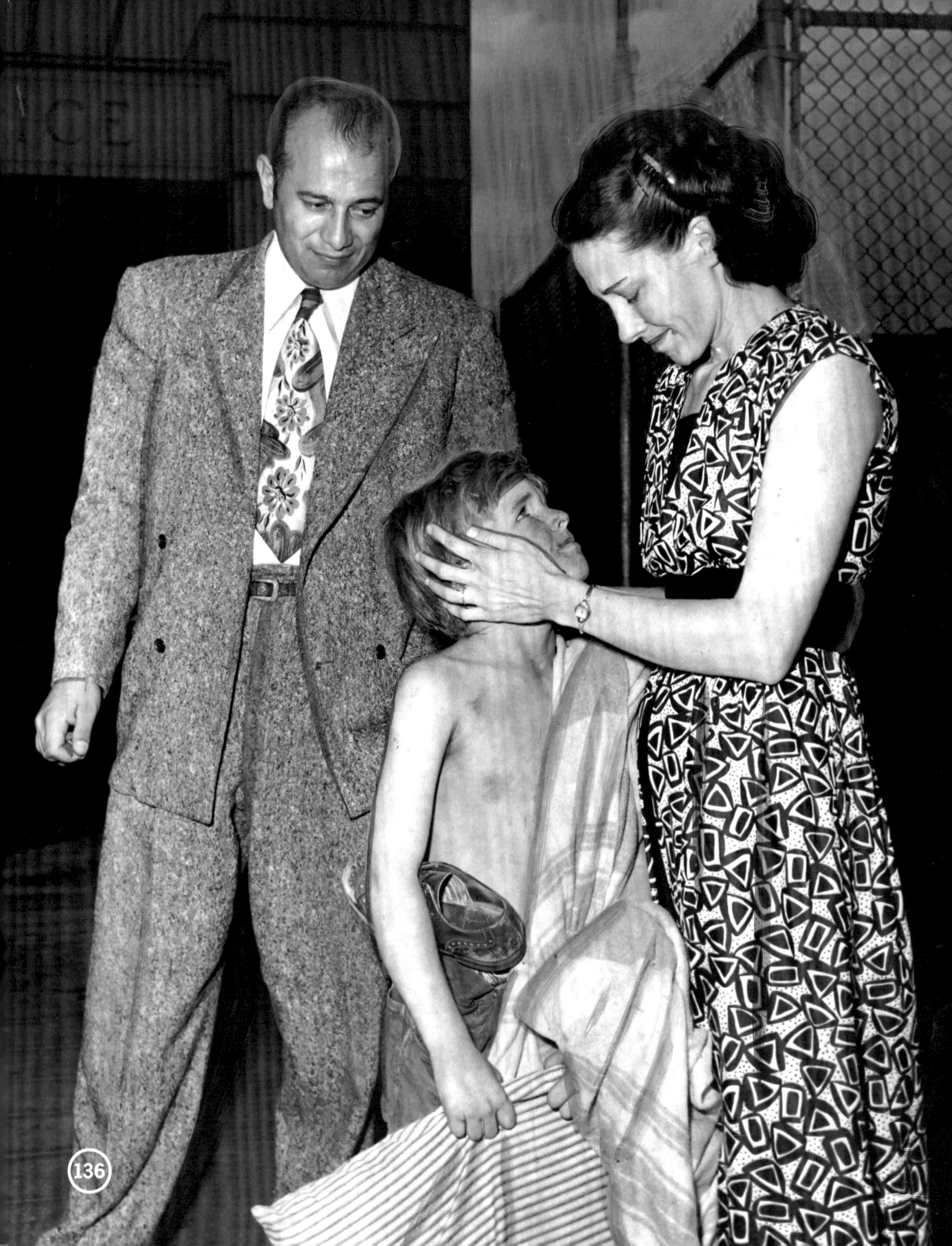

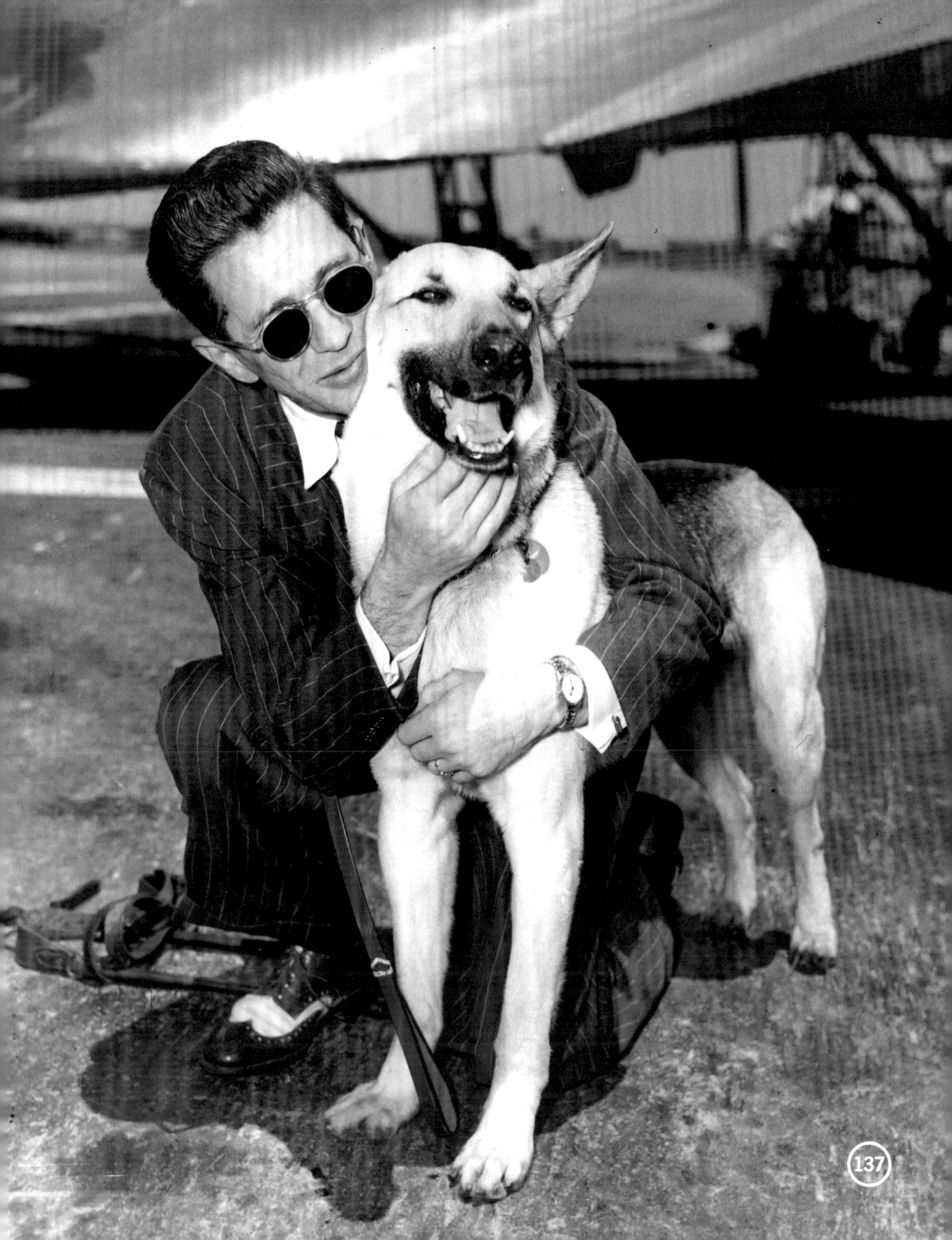

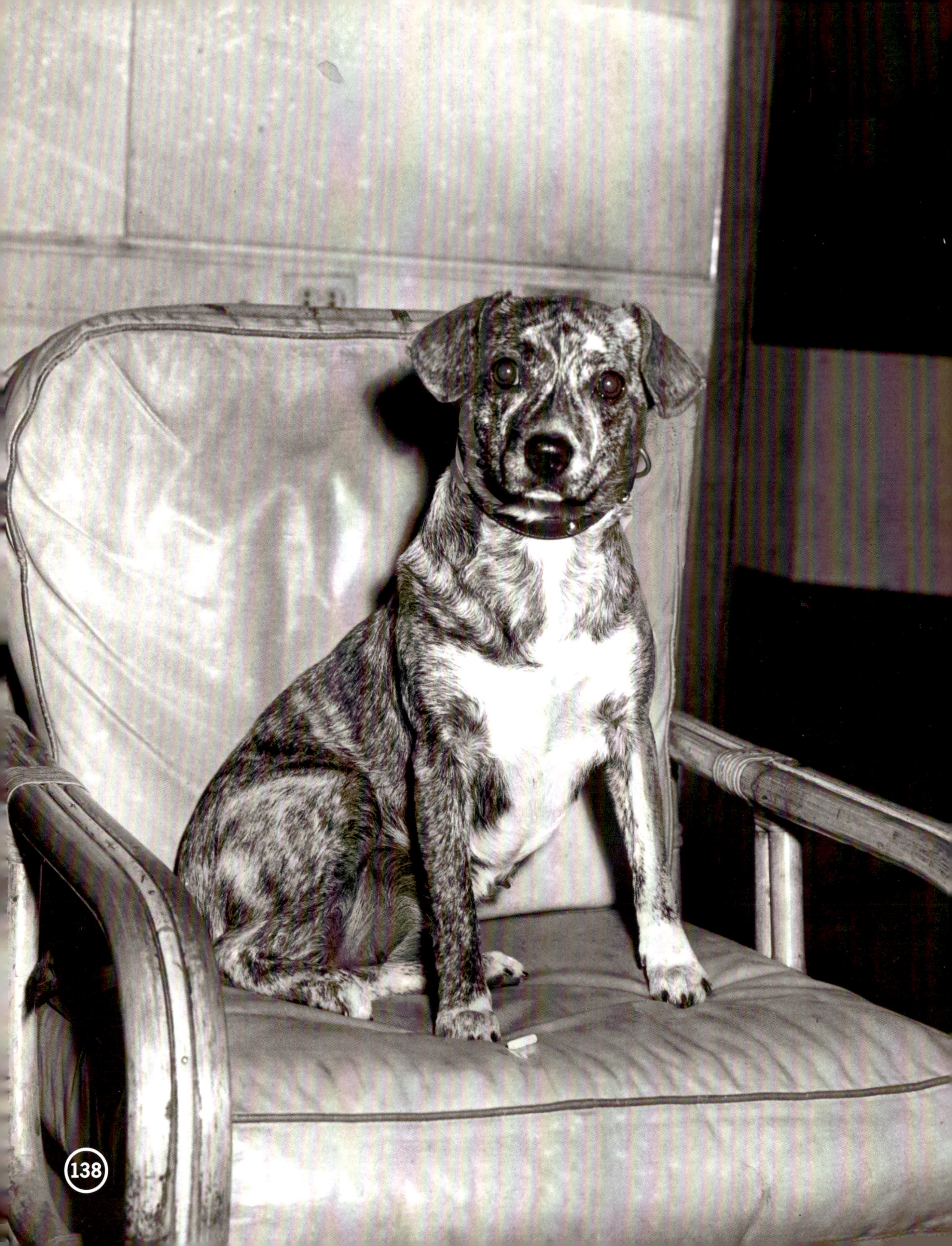

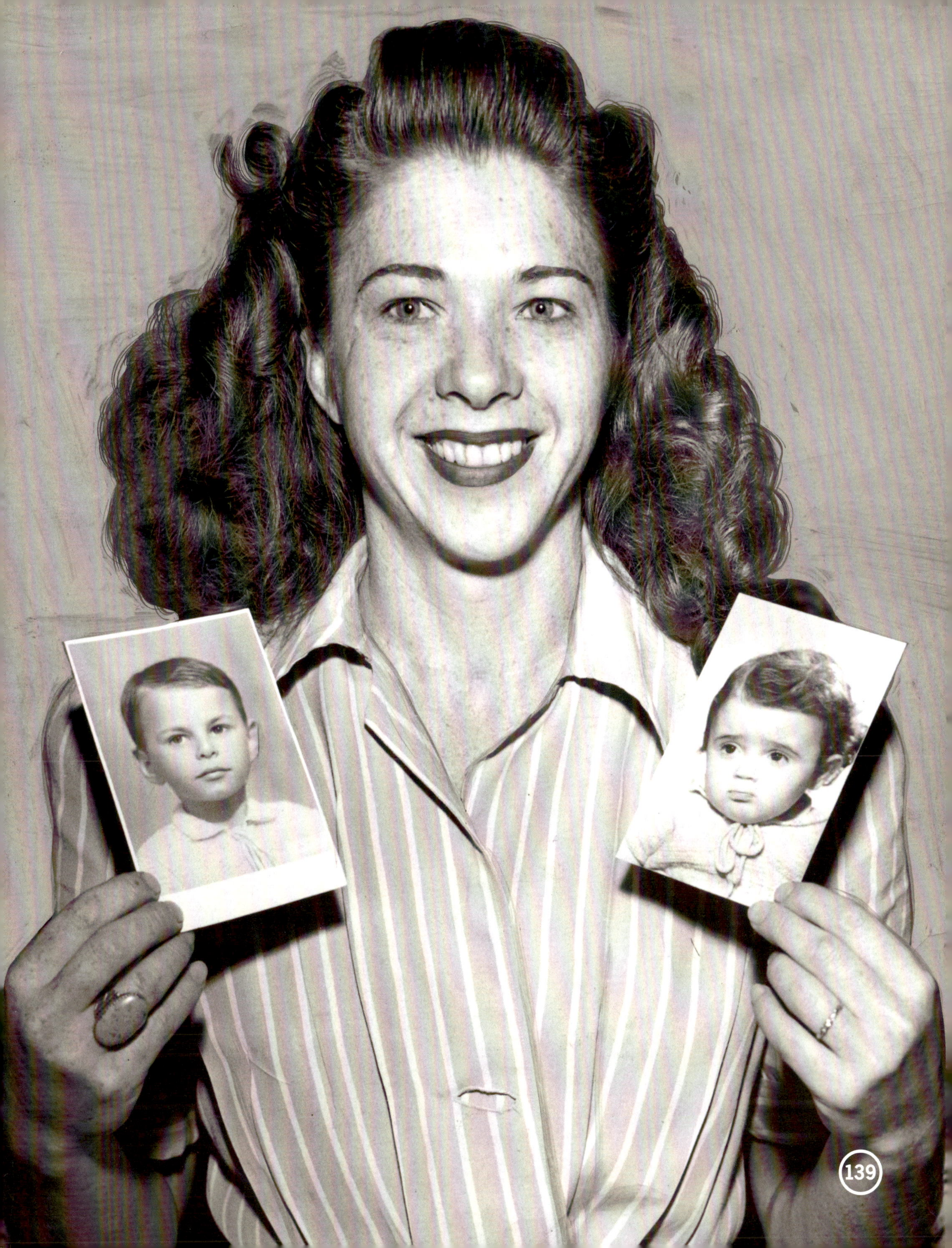

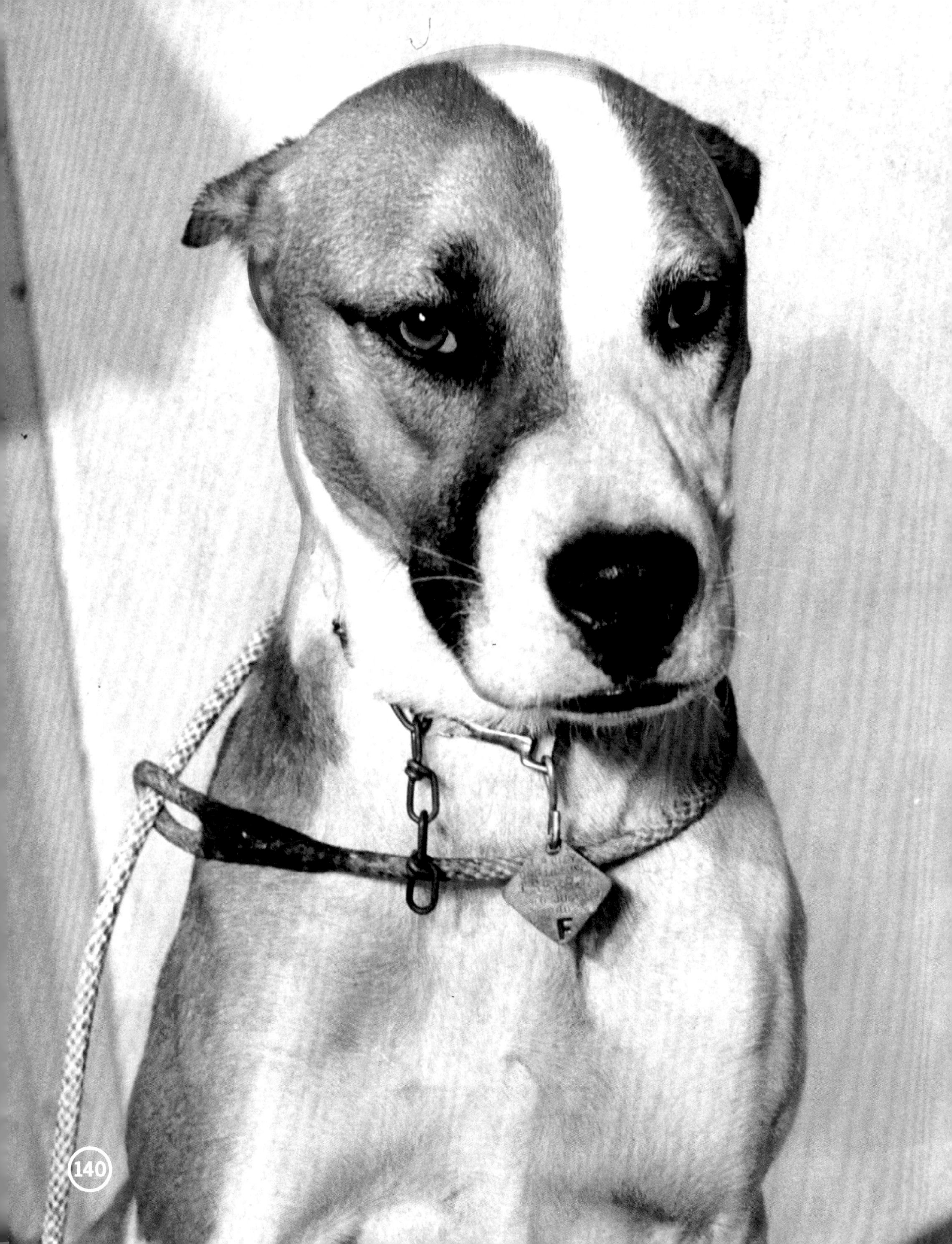

The photographs reproduced in LOCAL NEWS were selected from 2.2 million prints in the photo morgue of the LOS ANGELES HERALD EXAMINER at the LOS ANGELES PUBLIC LIBRARY. They are from the old files of the HERALD EXPRESS, an afternoon tabloid newspaper founded in 1931 by the legendary publisher William Randolph Hearst. At the end of the nineteenth century, Hearst and his archrival, newspaper publisher Joseph Pulitzer, came up with a successful approach to win over readers that was dubbed "yellow" journalism, which became known for its theatricality and sensationalism. Both men earned their reputations and fortunes producing newspapers that catered as much to the public's desire to escape from reality as their need to keep track of it.

The papers in Hearst's empire—which started in San Francisco, then spread to New York, Los Angeles, and elsewhere—appealed to early twentieth-century readers looking for escape from the monotony of their everyday lives. Some of Hearst's most popular papers were called tabloids because they were small, easily handled, and could be read quickly on crowded mass transportation in growing urban centers. Other larger-sized newspapers,

AFTER

called broadsheets, simply took on the aggressive tone and formulaic content of the tabloids. Regardless of the paper's scale, the impact of Hearst papers was huge. They spread the kind of news that focused on extreme, dramatic, and sentimental stories that the public could identify with and be entertained by. Tales of natural disasters, crimes petty or outrageous, freak accidents, police roundups, drug busts, unimaginable hardships, and all sorts of edgy and immoral behaviors were eagerly anticipated by devoted readers, more so than information about local political, civic, or cultural events. And, whenever possible, articles that explored the bizarre, the unexpected, and the erotic were made even juicier with eye-catching photographic images as attention-getting as they were informative.

In a city with six newspapers competing for the same audience, the HERALD EXPRESS (before it merged with another of Hearst's papers, the LOS ANGELES EXAMINER, in 1962) followed tabloid traditions established by East Coast papers like the NEW YORK DAILY NEWS. Front pages featured screaming headlines that pitched stories for all they were worth. Scandals, like that surrounding the HOUSE OF HORROR, and crimes dubbed with catchy names, like the BLACK DAHLIA MURDER, mesmerized the public and could be stretched out for days, weeks, or even years. The public quickly grew addicted to the rhythm of fever-pitched, episodic reporting. They feasted on a daily diet of punchy pictures that spread from the front page through the interior, across the centerfold, and out to the back cover. Stories were short, with local news taking precedence over national or international events. On every pulpy newsprint page, the emphasis was on the "personality" elements of every story. The same audience that bought one hundred million movie tickets weekly and eagerly demanded to see heroes and heroines in newsreels and feature films soon came to expect that equally dramatic pictures would illustrate the stories they read every day.

Editors and photographers who worked for the HERALD EXPRESS, and later the HERALD EXAMINER, obliged their audience of women, "men on the street," blue-collar workers, and immigrants. When there was no substantial news to be covered on any given day, a city the size of Los Angeles had enough bizarre and wacky photo-ops, eccentric characters, and offbeat happenings that made for compelling stories and mesmerizing pictures. Staff photographers lurked in courthouse vestibules, waiting to catch glimpses of well-dressed divorcees or suspects shielding their faces with coat lapels. They'd routinely grab their big cameras and chase cops to the scenes of crimes, hoping to find bodies, blood, and photogenic pieces of evidence. And if the pictures they brought back didn't have enough visual

WORD

impact, they handed them over to picture editors, who would crop or collage them to punch up their inherent drama. In the world of tabloid journalism, pictures didn't have to bear the burden of telling the whole truth; they just had to attract attention from across the street. No one gave a second thought to turning prints over to retouchers who'd paint in the highlights that would make pictures jump off the page, or paint out whatever, or whomever, might be distracting for readers ever eager to see photographs of people less fortunate than themselves.

That's how raucous pictures—of losers, loose women, and pathetic, hurt children; harshly lit, shot-from-below views of neighborhood crooks and villains; sentimental snaps of pets lost and found; and photographic evidence of every kind of passion, fate, and criminality— became a staple in the visual diet of mid-century Angelinos. And they were satisfying until urban sprawl made afternoon delivery of newspapers difficult, and television, with its own emphasis on local news, became so compelling that it brought the era of the tabloid to a less than sensational end.

—MARVIN HEIFERMAN AND CAROLE KISMARIC

The photographs in this book are from the **HERALD EXAMINER COLLECTION** at the **LOS ANGELES PUBLIC LIBRARY.** This archive of 2.2 million photographs includes images from the **HERALD EXPRESS** and the **HERALD EXAMINER,** the paper that came into being after the Herald merged with another Hearst newspaper, the Examiner, in 1962. The photographs reproduced in this volume are all from the **HERALD EXPRESS,** the evening paper that Angelinos enjoyed for three decades for its lively coverage of the local news.

All efforts have been made to identify the photographers and to clear rights to the photographs in **LOCAL NEWS.** Should additional information come to light it will be included in future editions.

Producers: **MARVIN HEIFERMAN** and **CAROLE KISMARIC**
Project Editor: **AKIKO TAKANO**
Editorial Assistants: **ELENA RITCHIE, RACHEL RANDOLPH**
Design: **BUREAU** (NYC)

ACKNOWLEDGMENTS
Heartfelt thank-you's to the following people at the Los Angeles Public Library: **CAROLYN KOZO COLE, GLEN CREASON, DAVID GOODMAN, FONTAYNE HOLMES, SUSAN KENT, MATTHEW MATTSON,** and **JANE NOWAK.** Thanks also to **MAURICE BERGER, ANDY CAPELLI, LAURA CITRANO, SHARON GALLAGHER, CINDY HELLER, AVERY LOZADA, DONALD MOFFETT,** and **BILL ROBINSON** for their help and support.

Published in 1999 by

D.A.P./DISTRIBUTED ART PUBLISHERS, INC.
155 Sixth Avenue
New York, N.Y. 10013
Tel: (212) 627-1999   Fax: (212) 627-9484

ISBN 1-891024-13-2
Printed and bound in Italy by **CENTRO GRAFICO RICORDI**

LOCAL NEWS is produced by **LOOKOUT**
1024 Avenue of the Americas
New York, N.Y. 10018
Tel: (212) 221-6463

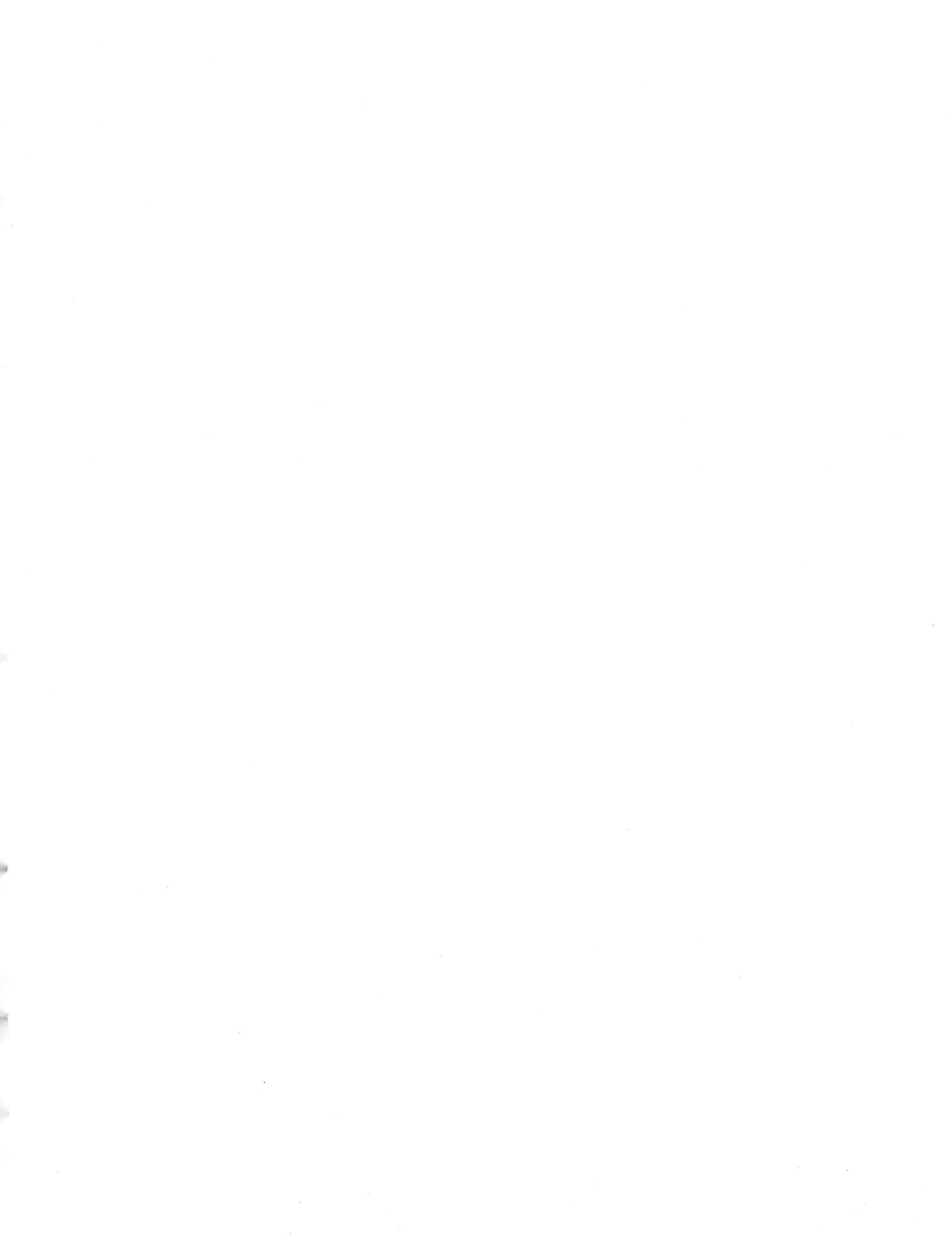